Cambridge Elements ≡

Elements in Development Economics
Series Editor-in-Chief
Kunal Sen
UNU-WIDER and University of Manchester

THE 1918–20 INFLUENZA PANDEMIC

A Retrospective in the Time of COVID-19

Prema-chandra Athukorala
Australian National University

Chaturica Athukorala
Canberra Hospital

Shaftesbury Road, Cambridge CB2 8EA, United Kingdom

One Liberty Plaza, 20th Floor, New York, NY 10006, USA

477 Williamstown Road, Port Melbourne, VIC 3207, Australia

314–321, 3rd Floor, Plot 3, Splendor Forum, Jasola District Centre, New Delhi – 110025, India

103 Penang Road, #05–06/07, Visioncrest Commercial, Singapore 238467

Cambridge University Press is part of Cambridge University Press & Assessment, a department of the University of Cambridge.

We share the University's mission to contribute to society through the pursuit of education, learning and research at the highest international levels of excellence.

www.cambridge.org
Information on this title: www.cambridge.org/9781009336086

DOI: 10.1017/9781009336062

First published 2022

A catalogue record for this publication is available from the British Library.

ISBN 978-1-009-33608-6 Paperback
ISSN 2755-1601 (online)
ISSN 2755-1598 (print)

Cambridge University Press & Assessment has no responsibility for the persistence or accuracy of URLs for external or third-party internet websites referred to in this publication and does not guarantee that any content on such websites is, or will remain, accurate or appropriate.

The 1918–20 Influenza Pandemic

A Retrospective in the Time of COVID-19

Elements in Development Economics

DOI: 10.1017/9781009336062
First published online: November 2022

Prema-chandra Athukorala
Australian National University

Chaturica Athukorala
Canberra Hospital

Author for correspondence: Prema-chandra.athukorala@anu.edu.au

Abstract: The pandemic of 1918–20 – commonly known as the Spanish Flu – infected over a quarter of the world's population and killed over 50 million people. It is by far the greatest humanitarian disaster caused by an infectious disease in modern history. Epidemiologists and health scientists often draw on this experience to set the plausible upper bound (the 'worst-case scenario') on future pandemic mortality. The purpose of this study is to piece together and analyse the scattered multi-disciplinary literature on the pandemic in order to place debates on the evolving course of the current COVID-19 crisis in historical perspective. The analysis focuses on the changing characteristics of pathogens and disease over time, the institutional factors that shaped the global spread, the demographic and socio-economic consequences, and pharmaceutical and non-pharmaceutical responses to the pandemic. This title is also available as Open Access on Cambridge Core.

Keywords: Spanish flu, 1918–20 influenza pandemic, COVID-19 pandemic, demographic change, fetal origin hypothesis, economic growth, equity, pharmaceutical intervention, non-pharmaceutical intervention

ISBNs: 9781009336086 (PB), 9781009336062 (OC)
ISSNs: 2755-1601 (online), 2755-1598 (print)

Contents

1 Why Revisit the 1918–20 Influenza Pandemic?

Since a cluster of infections was reported in the Hunan Seafood Wholesale Market in China on 30 December 2019, the SARS-COV-2 virus has spread at an alarming speed in every continent. The global spread of the virus was so fast that on 11 March 2020, the World Health Organization (WHO) named the virus outbreak the 'COVID-19 pandemic'. As of this writing (in late September 2021), cases of infection exceeded 242.4 million and fatalities had surpassed 4.9 million.[1] So far there are only three sovereign states that have no confirmed cases.[2] Thanks to marshalling of scientific resources, large-scale testing, and social distancing, some countries were able to contain the spread of the virus by late 2020, but an outbreak of a new, more virulent variant of the virus has trashed hope of an early ending to the pandemic. The spread of the virus is accelerating in developing countries, where both pharmaceutical and non-pharmaceutical defences are far less effective, and poverty and comorbidity (prevalence of other infectious diseases) provide ideal conditions for rapid spread. Because the world economy has become irrevocably interdependent, no country can win the fight against the virus on its own. Baring the possible yet unpredictable situation of the virus running its own course, the pandemic will end only when the infection rate is brought down to a manageable level and most of the world population is vaccinated.

Pandemics are defining events in human history with lasting effects on the economy and society. History may not repeat itself, but historical information offers valuable insights that are highly relevant to today's concerns. It is important to set pandemics against a historical background and discuss the implications in terms of continuing changes within the context of a shifting global landscape. Reasoning by historical analogy does not, of course, provide definitive lessons but helps to identify areas where more thinking and research are required for designing evidence-based public policy intervention.

The purpose of this Element is to piece together and analyse the scattered multi-disciplinary literature on the Great Influenza Pandemic of 1918–20 (commonly known as the Spanish Flu) to place in historical perspective the current debates on the evolving course of the COVID-19 pandemic and its socio-economic implications. The 1918–20 pandemic, the deadliest humanitarian disaster in modern history with a death toll of around 50 million worldwide,

---

[1] The Johns Hopkins University, the Center for Systems Science and Engineering's COVID-19 Dashboard (https://coronavirus.jhu.edu/map.html).

[2] Two tiny island nations in Oceania (Tuvalu and Tonga) and Turkmenistan. Turkmenistan, with a population of about 6 million, has not officially reported any cases of COVID-19 infection. However, there are reports of more deaths from acute respiratory illnesses in the country than normal, and all neighbouring countries have reported cases of COVID-19 (Yaylymova, 2020)

is considered by many epidemiologists and public health authorities as the 'worst-case scenario' in developing pandemic preparedness plans.

The 1918–20 pandemic and the COVID-19 pandemic are caused by two unrelated viruses: the H1NI strain of avian influenza and the severe acute respiratory syndrome coronavirus, SARS-COV-2. However, their transmission is similar, occurring by inhaling droplets generated by an infected individual. Both viruses have the inherent feature of a high mutation rate with the possibility of efficient transmission from person to person and mutating to become more virulent (Petersen et al., 2020; Wang et al., 2020). Therefore, as public health crises they are strikingly similar in their clinical, pathological, and epidemiological features, and in civic, public health, and medical responses used to control them.

For over seven decades, the 1918–20 pandemic remained a 'forgotten human catastrophe' in social sciences and public policy discourse, for several related reasons (Bolanovsky & Erreygers, 2021; Burnet, 1979; Phillips, 2004; The Economist, 2020a, 2020b). First, the pandemic was overshadowed by the First World War (WW1): the first two waves of the pandemic occurred in the final year of WW1. In the warring nations, other than the United States, the death rate of the pandemic was much smaller than the war death rate, and the trauma of the war and the subsequent jubilant armistice perhaps overwhelmed the memories of the pandemic in people's minds.[3] Second, given the variety of censorship measures introduced by the warring nations during WW1 to keep the spirit of the population high and the rudimentary state of the worldwide mass media, the global scale of the pandemic would not have been immediately available to local experience.[4] Therefore, at a time when, outbreaks of infectious diseases were a recurrent feature of life (Fan et al., 2018), the pandemic would have been perceived as yet another outbreak. Third, given the Eurocentric nature of scholarship during the colonial era, socio-economic implications of the pandemic for present-day developing countries (most of which were colonies of the Western nations) that bore the brunt of the death toll remained virtually beyond the focus of public policy debate and scholarship. Colonial historiographers have been for the most part, if not exclusively,

---

[3] WW1, which started on 28 July 1914 and ended in November 1918, claimed 10 million lives as the direct result of warfare. About 50 million people died as a result of the pandemic. The US, which joined the War only at its final stage, suffered 117 thousand direct war casualties compared to over 550 thousand pandemic deaths. In other warring nations the number of war casualties far exceeded pandemic deaths. (Compare pandemic deaths reported in the Appendix with war death given at www.britannica.com/event/World-War-I).

[4] Byerly (2005) argues that the US medical officers and military leaders, given their helplessness to control influenza, began to downplay the epidemic as a significant event, in effect erasing this dramatic story of the pandemic from the American historical memory.

concerned with the interests of the colonial power, rather than with those of the colonial inhabitants. Finally, economists remained virtually silent about the pandemic presumably because the pandemic-induced recession in the United States and other countries was sharp but short-lived and lurked in the background of massive war devastation.[5] Consequently, the study of the pandemic remained largely a by-product of works by epidemiologists and virologists, whose prime goal was to discover why it had been so lethal and to find ways to prevent the recurrence of a pandemic of similar proportions, and the ancillary writings of a few medical historians.

In contrast to the remarkable silence of social sciences and public policy discourse, the pandemic was widely discussed in both medical journals (such as *The Lancet, the British Medical Journal*, and *US Public Health Reports*) and general science journals (such as *Science* and *Scientific America*), as epidemiologists were alarmed by the scale and seriousness of the pandemic. Presumably, media restrictions were not applied to these professional journals because they were not opened to public discourse. However, even in medical research, interest in the pandemic waned from about the late 1940s because of the growing complacency rooted in medical advances that allayed fears about a comparable future lethal pandemic. For instance, in the early 1950s, Sir MacFarlane Burnet, the Australian pioneer in modern influenza research and Nobel Laureate, wrote in the second edition of his magnum opus of infectious disease, 'In many ways one can think of the middle of the twentieth century as the end of one of the most important social revolutions in history, the virtual elimination of infectious diseases as a significant factor in social life' (Burnet, 1953: 3). As he predicted, the death toll of the 1957 Asian flu pandemic and 1968 Hong Kong Influenza pandemic were not higher than those of any 'ordinary' influenza year, even though there was no reason for believing that the virus was of lesser virulence than the 1918–20 virus, presumably because of advances in medicine in the intervening 40 years. Moreover, by then the world had conquered polio, nearly eradicated smallpox and assembled an arsenal of antibiotic perforations. Twenty years later, the fourth and last edition of the book, therefore, concluded, 'To write about infectious disease is almost to write of something that has passed into history . . . [T]he most likely forecast about the future of infectious disease is that it will be very dull' (Burnet & White, 1972: 263).

---

[5] None of the major economic journals published an article on the pandemic during 1918–21 other than just one article in the *American Economic Review* (March 1920, 285), which referred to it only metaphorically (Bolanovsky & Erreygers (2021: 94). A celebrated book on business cycles covering this period inferred that 'in view of the pandemic's *exceptional brevity and moderate amplitude,* its failures to register in annual summaries is not surprising' (emphasis added) (Burns & Mitchell, 1946: 109).

By the late twentieth century, it seemed to some that the world had reached 'the end of medical history' (Hampton, 1998).

There has been a revival of multi-disciplinary interests in infectious diseases and learning from the 1918–20 pandemic over the past three decades (Murray et al., 2006; Osterholm, 2005; Osteholm & Olshaker, 2017; Phillips, 2014). This was propelled by a significant increase in morbidity and mortality during the normal flu season in countries in the northern hemisphere and, more importantly, the outbreak of several influenza epidemics, which had the potential to gain pandemic proportions around the world at a remarkably shorter frequency. These included the outbreak of Hong Kong flu (1997), the severe acute respiratory syndrome (SARS) (2002–03), the Middle East respiratory syndrome (MERS) (2012), and swine flu (2008–10) (da Costa et al., 2020; Ewald, 2011; Garrett, 2005). The threat of a 1918–20-like severity pandemic received attention in medical journals in the 2010s by reports of five epidemics in China caused by an Asian lineage 'type A influenza strain'[6] that posed pandemic potential during 2013–17 (Jester et al., 2018).

There is growing concern among epidemiologists about increased probability of zoonotic transfer of pathogen to human because of the intensification of food-animal production (Osterholm & Olshaker, 2017: Chapter 18). Nearly all of the emerging infectious disease episodes around the world have come from human interaction with the animal world (Gregoer, 2020: Chapter 2). These diseases are caused by viruses which find their natural home in birds, mostly fowl, and only infect humans when they cross the species barrier, sometimes directly and sometimes moving through an intermediary species such as pigs or horses. The rapid expansion of modern confinement food-animal production and the establishment of many millions of firms around the world, has given the viruses ample opportunity to find a suitable host for their evolutionary process.

The fear of a coming influenza pandemic has motivated epidemiologists and health economists to draw on the 1918–20 pandemic as the worst-case planning scenario to set a plausible upper bound. For instance, Murray et al. (2006), by relating mortality records of 27 countries during the 1918–20 pandemic to their population in 2004, predicted a death toll of 62 million deaths of a future pandemic of similar magnitude. An update of this estimate to the 2017 world population using data for 47 countries by Barro et al. (2020) suggests a death total of 150 million. A comprehensive survey of influenza epidemics by two prominent epidemiologists infers that 'even with modern antiviral and antibacterial drugs, vaccines and preventive knowledge, the returning of a pandemic virus equivalent in pathogenicity to the virus of 1918 would kill over 100

---

[6] The influenza strains that cause influenza pandemics in both animals and humans.

million people worldwide' (Taubenberger & Morens, 2006). Health administrators in many countries have begun to draw on this information when developing pandemic preparedness plans (Chandra & Christensen, 2017; Gulland, 2016; Richard et al., 2009; Moxnes & Christophersen, 2008; Nickol & Kindrachuk, 2019).

After the onset of the COVID-19 pandemic, commentators have begun to refer to the 1918–20 pandemic when seeking a historical analogy. The evolving body of knowledge on the propagation of the COVID-19 pandemic and the concern about a possible second wave are heavily based on its historiography. (Ferguson et al., 2020; Jones, 2020; Wang et al., 2020; World Economic Forum, 2020). A number of studies have emerged comparing and contrasting the two pandemics focussing on what lessons we have learned and how we are applying these lessons to the challenges of COVID-19 (Arthi & Parman, 2021; Beach et al., 2020; Morens et al., 2021; Osterholm & Olshaker, 2020; Taubenberger & Moran, 2020).

This Element begins with a stage-setting discussion on the origin and global propagation of the 1918–20 pandemic (Section 2). Section 3 provides a broad brush of the pandemic humanitarian disaster and the demographic profile of casualties using a synthesis of data compiled from a comprehensive survey of the literature. Section 4 surveys the geographical patterns of pandemic mortality. Policy responses to the pandemic are discussed in Section 5. Section 6 examines socio-economic implications of the pandemic. The final section makes some concluding remarks on lessons from the pandemic that can be applied when navigating the current COVID-19 pandemic.

2 Origin and Global Spread

The geographical origin of the virus that caused the 1918–20 pandemic remains unknown. The first recorded case of fatality in the 1918–20 pandemic was in April 1918 at the Funston Army Camp in eastern Kansas, USA, which fed a constant stream of men to other military bases in America and Europe during WW1. However, there is no absolute certainty as to where the virus originated.

In the first comprehensive epidemiological survey of the pandemic sponsored by the American Medical Association, Edwin Jordan (1927) identified three possible sites: Haskell, Kansas; British military camps in Great Britain and France, and China. Based on a survey of medical journals, he noted that there was evidence of unusually virulent respiratory disease in all three locations in advance of the first wave of the pandemic. However, based on a public health report from Haskell, Kansas, dated March 1918, he conjectured that the disease might have first appeared in Haskell and then transmitted to the army camps and spread from west to east across the United States and then across the Atlantic to Europe.

Taking cue from Jordan, medical historian John M. Barry (2004a, 2004b) traced the origin of the pandemic to Haskell County in northwest Kansas where 'farmers lived in close proximity to pigs and fowl'. These findings, based on a study of US Public Health Service reports, suggest a reported case of infection there in March and the arrival of recruits from Haskell County in the nearby Camp Funston between 28 February and 2 March 1918. From there the virus spread to the other army camps across the United States and later across the world with the arrival of American troops in Europe. However, the exact zoonotic origin of the virus is unknown: avian and swine origins have been proposed. It is difficult to know the exact origin of any pandemic disease because infectious agents arise via the host switching from an animal to a human, after which successful adaptation facilitates human to human transmission.

The virologist John Oxford and this research associates have come up with evidence in support of the European origin of the virus (Oxford, 2001; Oxford et al., 2002). They noted specific outbreaks of a respiratory disease (called epidemic bronchitis, rather than influenza at the time) by the British army's doctors at two army bases in England (Aldershot, South-West of London) and France (Ètaples) that prodded the first wave of the pandemic (the years 1915–17). Their thesis is that the peculiar conditions of trench warfare allowed the outbreak to emerge as a new pandemic virus, incubated by a lethal combination of gas, filth, overcrowding, and human cohabitation with livestock, especially pigs and fowl. Some of these earlier focal outbreaks occurred during the winter months when influenza was known to be in circulation and presented with a particular heliotrope cyanosis that was so prominent in clinical diagnosis during the world pandemic outbreak of 1918–19. Based on this evidence they postulated that the pandemic had its origins on the Western Front, and that WW1 was a contributor (Oxford et al., 2002).

Jordan (1927) documented the views of some contemporary writers that the flu had been brought to Europe by the Chinese Labour Corps (CLCs).[7] However, he stopped short of exploring this possibility because of the absence of epidemiological records from China and the absence of access to Chinese language material. A number of more recent studies have built on Jordan's work to shed further light on the Chinese origin hypothesis (Humphries, 2014; Langford, 2005; Shortridge, 1999). Shortridge (1999) argues that Southern

---

[7] The Chinese Labour Corps (CLCs) was a force of workers recruited by the British government in the First World War to perform support work and manual labour in order to free troops for front line duty. During 1917–18, 940,000 CLC workers moved from China across North America to Europe (Humphries, 2014).

China was the source of the virus. He comes up with this proposition by combining the evidence of the prevalence of influenza in Canton (now called Guangzhou in Guangdong Province) in Southern China throughout the early 1900s and the engagement of Chinese labourers who spoke Cantonese dialect of Guangdong province in constructing trenches around camps in Montreuil, France. Langford (2005) and Pettit & Bailie (2008) report evidence of a severe form of respiratory illness, with symptoms of approximating both pneumonic plague and 1918–20 influenza, circulating in the interior of China and cite mobilisation of the CLC as the main vector of transmitting the disease around the globe. Humphries (2014), argues that the Chinese origin hypothesis is the most convincing. Based on British and Canadian archival research relating to influenza in the Canadian Expeditionary Force and the movement of Chinese CLC workers via Vancouver, he pieced together an epidemiological chain from the interior of China to the battlefields of Europe. According to internal military correspondence studied by Humphries (2014), both Chinese and Western Officials involved in recruiting CLC labourers identified the disease that appeared among Chinese workers bound for Vancouver from the outbreak-affected regions in China as 1918–20 influenza rather than pneumonic flue.

The pandemic spread in distinct waves, with the number of waves and the timing of each varying among countries and regions. Countries in the northern hemisphere and Asian countries that sent troops to the war experienced three waves: March–August 1918, late August–December 1918, and early 1919 until about May 1919. In the first wave, the virus rapidly spread from Funston to other military bases in the United States during March 1918. The first outbreak in Europe occurred in Brest, France, in early April, where US troops embarked. From the European war front, the virus quickly spread from France to Britain, Italy, Spain, Germany, Russia, and other countries in Europe over the following two months. There were recorded cases of infection in India, China, Singapore, and Indonesia by late May through troop movements.

News of the flu and the ravages caused in the trenches of the Western Front and war camps in the United States remained censored in the United States and the warring nations to avoid damaging soldiers' morale. The media obtained news of the flu from war-neutral Spain where there was free media, even though the virus only reached there in May. Hence, the moniker 'Spanish Flu'[8] has stuck to the

---

[8] In 2015, the World Health Organization (WHO), in consultation and collaboration with the World Organisation for Animal Health (OIE) and the Food and Agriculture Organization (FAO), issued guidelines on *Best Practices for the Naming of New Human Infectious Diseases* with the aim to minimize unnecessary negative impact of disease names on trade, travel, tourism, or animal welfare and to avoid causing offence to any cultural, social, national, regional, professional, or ethnic groups. These guidelines, which we follow in this paper, stipulated that disease names

1918–20 pandemic to this day. The news from Spain added attraction in the media because Spanish King Alfonso XIII was infected with the virus, along with his prime minister and some members of the cabinet (Spinney, 2017).

The infection was mild in the first wave, and the death rate was similar to that of normal seasonal flu with old people and children especially at risk. However, by late August 1918, the virus had mutated to a more deadly and contagious form, instigating the deadly second wave in which adults between the ages of 20 to 40 were particularly susceptible. The three port cities – Freetown, Sierra Leon; Brest, France; and Boston, Massachusetts – were the initial hotspots. During the next three months, the disease swept not only North America and Europe but also the entire world as far as the Alaskan wilderness and the most remote islands of the Pacific (Burnet & Clark, 1942). October 1918 was the month with the highest fatality rate of the whole pandemic. The disease was of sufficient virulence to cause death within a few days of the development of symptoms (The Economist, 2018; Wever & van Bergen, 2014). However, many victims of the first wave had become immune to the virus and showed significant resistance to the second wave, providing strong evidence that the deadly virus was a variant of the first one (Gladwell, 1997; Taubenberger, 2003).

By December 1918, North America and most parts of Europe were free of flu. But a third wave struck in January 1919 when the world was still recovering from the second wave. The virus had mutated again and was less virulent than that encountered in the second wave but much more severe than that of the first wave. The third wave peaked in the United States and Europe in January and February when the Paris peace negotiations were underway. Some analysts treat the third wave as 'a normal series of trailer outcomes' (Patterson & Pyle, 1991: 4). However, there is strong evidence that it was clearly a continuation of the pandemic: 'the abnormally high proportion of deaths among young adults, a unique characteristics of the second wave (Section 7.1), continued right through the third wave' (Crosby, 2003: 203). According to most historical records, the pandemic was over in the northern hemisphere by May 1919. However, in some parts of the world (e.g., Scandinavia, some South Atlantic islands, Japan, and some Latin American countries) it persisted into 1920.

The timing of onset and duration of the pandemic varied significantly in the rest of the world. In India the pandemic began with the arrival of infected troops from Basra in Iraq in Bombay (now Mumbai) and Karachi in May–June 1918[9]

---

should not refer to specific places, people, animals, or food. www.who.int/ topics/infectious_di seases/naming-new-diseases/en/

[9] Around 1.5 million Indian servicemen (including 827 thousand fighting troops) played an important part in the WW1, servicing in almost every theatre of the war. The bulk of these servicemen came from villages scattered all over the Indian subcontinent (Morton-Jack, 2018).

(Arnold, 2019). The mild first wave lasted only about two months: by late July the pandemic was nearly over. Then the fatal second wave swept across India from September to early December 1918, with infected servicemen and servicemen retiring from the war front arriving home to their villages. Across the country, rural areas suffered as much as cities because many of the volunteer soldiers came from villages. The pandemic lasted in most provinces well into 1919 and gave high mortality in that year in Bengal and the United Provinces; local outbreaks continued throughout the country during the next two years (Sen, 1967).[10]

In Ceylon (Sri Lanka), the first cases of influenza appeared among workers in Colombo port in June 1918. Subsequently the disease entered the Island through the arrival of indentured labour from South India through Talaimannar in the North, which linked the colonial railway systems of the two countries (Chandra & Sarathchandra, 2014; Langford & Storey 1992).

In Southeast Asia, the virus came to the port of Singapore through troop movements in June 1918 and spread to the other Strait Settlements, Malaya and Indonesia through maritime and land routes (Lee et al., 2007; Liew, 2007). In Indonesia, the first case of infection was reported in July 1918, but the real onset of the pandemic was in September 1918. The impact was most intense during eight weeks from late October until early December 1918, and it took until September 1919 before the mortality rate returned to the levels of the 1912–17 average (van der Eng, 2020). The virus was brought to Thailand in October 1918 by troops retiring from France.[11] The disease spread from the harbour city in southern Thailand throughout the entire country and subsided by March 1919 (Thongcharoen, 2017).

The virus did not reach Japan or countries and territories under Japanese colonial rule (Korea, Taiwan, Kuang-Tun Leased Territory, Sakhalin Island, and South Sea Islands) until October 1918. The first deadly wave there was from November 1918 to January 1919, and the second wave started in December 1919 and lasted in some parts of the country as long as June 1920 (Hayami, 2015).

Thanks to its remote location, the news of the pandemic reached Australia, New Zealand, and the Pacific Islands in late August 1918. Australia managed to avoid an outbreak until early 1919 (when the third wave set in) through stringent marine quarantine (see Section 4). The virus reached Latin America belatedly presumably because it was not significantly exposed to the movements of military personnel during WW1 (Chowell et al., 2011, 2014). There is also

---

[10] Based on data from Government of India (1924).

[11] Thailand remained an Independent country throughout the colonial era, but it joined the Allied forces at the final stage of WW1 to honour its commitment to Britain under the Bowring Treaty of 1855.

evidence that the pandemic lasted longer there: in the Peruvian capital Lima, the pandemic peaked in early 1920 and lingered through 1921.

The pandemic spread in the African continent in three waves between March 1918 and early 1919 (Ohadike, 1991; Pankhurst, 1977; Patterson, 1983; Patterson & Pyle, 1983; Phillips, 1988, 2017; Ranger, 1992). The first wave began with the arrival of the virus in Freetown (Sierra Leone) on a Royal Navy Warship (in March 1918). It diffused relatively slowly into the Sierra Leone hinterland but spread rapidly through coastal shipping to Dakar in Senegal, and Cape Town and Durbin in South Africa, and from there to Natal, Zululand and the mines of Transvaal in the South African interior. Most of the countries in sub-Saharan Africa were not affected by this first wave. The second wave entered Africa with the military men returning from the trenches of WW1 in September 1918 through three seaports, Freetown, Cape Town (South Africa), and Mombasa (Kenya).[12] The mild third wave began in early 1919, and lingered on throughout the year and perhaps beyond in some parts of the continent. The pandemic spread along the coast and far inland (through the newly constructed colonial transport networks and did not reach some of the remote northern territories until about March 1919. The prime vectors on land were recently demobilised soldiers and carriers/porters, families fleeing infected towns, railway personnel, and migrant workers from nine compounds. The pandemic ravaged the continent far and wide, from Dakar to Mombasa and from Cap Town to Congo. There is evidence that countries that were exposed to the first mild wave gained considerable immunity in the second wave (Patterson, 1983; Phillips, 2017).

The 1918–20 pandemic was the first historical illustration of 'the unification of the globe by disease' in human history (Ladurie, 1981). At the height of the second wave in October 1918, the disease had spread to all human-inherited parts of the world up to the Alaskan wilderness, other than New Guinea and a few other isolated places. The two other mega pandemics of human history are the Plague of Justinian (around 540–541 AD) and the Black Death (bubonic plague) of 1347–59. Though as deadly as they were, these pandemics were largely confined to geographically contiguous countries and countries linked by mainland trade routes (Alfani & Murphy, 2017; Scheidel, 2017). Thus, even at a time when naval transport was the sole conduit of human interaction across seas, the 1918–19 pandemic vividly illustrated that the 'whole civilised world can be regarded as a single epidemiological unit as far as influenza is concerned' (Burnet, 1953: 285). The initial spread was related to wartime accommodation

---

[12] During WW1, Britain mobilised over 60 thousand combat troops and about 1 million conscripted labourers for non-combat tasks ('Career Corps') from its own colonies and also from German and Portuguese colonies in East Africa, and from South Africa (Strachan, 2004).

and movement of military personnel. However, the severity of the impact was not related to a country's combatant status: 'mortality caused by a deadly pathogen is partly a reflection of the social and political order it attacks' (Ferguson, 2021: 3).

Another important trait of the 1918–20 pandemic, which has remained a puzzle to both medical researchers and historians, is its brevity (Ranger, 2003). As noted, the pandemic dissipated within a period of less than one year in Europe and North America. Even in the global periphery, it did not last more than one and a half years after allowing for the time lag involved in spread. What explains this sudden disappearance of the virus?

The often-held media view is that people would have gotten accustomed to living with the disease (Kolata, 2020). This is, however, not consistent with the available vital statistics. In all countries for which data are available, the death rate had returned to the average pre-pandemic levels after the 'recorded' ending dates. Because the pathogen causing the disease was not even known at the time, it is certain that the pandemic did not end as a result of medical intervention. Another possibility is the virus stopped presumably because it ran out of human fuel: that is, it ran out of accessible people to infect. Those who lived through it were immune to reinfection or dead (Gregoer, 2020). Perhaps the most convincing explanation is that the spread of the virus ran its *natural* course within that short period because of its unique genetic characteristics that still remain a puzzle to epidemiologists (Taubenberger, 2003). A survey of historical records dating back to the early middle ages also suggests that epidemics and pandemics were 'not spontaneously persistent' and most of them were short-lived (Ladurie, 1981: 37).

3 Mortality: Count and Demographic Profile

3.1 Counting the Disaster

There are three commonly used measures for assessing the humanitarian effect of an infectious disease: morbidity – individuals in the population who are infected with the virus (the 'attack rate'); mortality – the number of deaths among the infected; and case mortality – deaths (fatality) among positive cases. Our knowledge of the 1918–20 pandemic is largely confined to data on mortality rates. Early estimates of pandemic mortality were based on administrative records and media reports with 'informed' adjustment for underreporting. For some countries, pandemic fatality data are informed guesses rather than the result of an analysis of available data. Most of the recent estimates are 'excess mortality' calculations based on comparison of recorded mortality during the pandemic years with those for a selected number of pre- and post-pandemic years (the number of people who died over and above what might have been expected in a 'normal' [non-pandemic] year). A number of countries in Eastern Europe, Arab Middle East, and Africa are not covered in these estimates because of the unavailability of data. Data on morbidity and case mortality are sparse and even less reliable.

Pandemic mortality data, even in countries with vital statistics recording systems, are not accurate, and the degree of accuracy varies among countries. At the initial stage of an outbreak of an influenza pandemic, there can be contamination of pandemic deaths with deaths because diagnostic criteria for distinguishing influenza and pneumonia are vague. Also, the magnitude of the pandemic in itself could distract accurate recording because physicians and nurses had much more compelling demands than to keep accurate records. Defining the pandemic's duration (when it exactly started and/or stopped) is also arbitrary. In most countries the available data from administrative records are concentrated heavily in the last third of 1918 and the first half of 1919. For instance, in 1918, the area from which the US Census Bureau received transcriptions of all death certificates contained only 77.8 per cent of the total estimated population of the nation (Barry, 2004a).

For these reasons, the best way to get a more accurate picture is to look at excess mortality (Aron & Muelbauer, 2020). It is important to note. however, that excess mortality estimates capture both mortality of the pandemic and depressed fertility through moral restraint during the pandemic. The extent to which the estimated 'excess' is contaminated with other deaths could vary from country to country depending in particular on comorbidity (concurrent susceptibility to other diseases). Even after allowing for this limitation, the accuracy of excess mortality estimates is subject to the quality and coverage of the vital statistic collection systems in any given country.

In this section, we treat the available estimates at face value to understand the order of magnitude of the death toll and inter-country differences. The first estimate of the global death toll of the 1918–20 pandemic was by Jordan (1927). This study estimated the global death toll at 27.6 million (Table 1). This estimate was based on data from North America, Europe, and a few large British colonies for which some administrative records of mortality were available. In the first major review of the literature on influenza epidemics, Burnet and Clark (1942) stated that the figure could be anywhere between 25 million and 50 million. Patterson and Pyle (1991: 15) came up with an estimate of 24.7 million to 39.3 million while suggesting a 'conservative total of roughly 30 million victims'. Johnson and Muller (2002) updated Patterson and Pyle's figures from 32.4 million to 41.3 million. This was based on a comprehensive synthesis of the literature up to about 1998. Johnson and Muller present these figures with the

Table 1 Global deaths of the 1918–20 influenza pandemic

Study	Number of countries covered	Deaths (millions)	Death rate (%)[a]
Jordan (1927)	?	21.6	1.2
Burnet and White (1972)	?	25.0–50.0	1.4–2.7
Patterson and Pyle (1991)[b]	44	24.7–39.3	1.3–2.2
Johnson and Mueller (2002)[c]	57	32.7–42.6	1.8–2.3
Barro et al. (2020)[d]	48	40	2.2
This study (Appendix)[e]	72	34.5–43.9	1.9–2.4

Note: [a] the world population (2017) used in calculating the death rate is 1,832 million (from the UN population database, www.un.org/en/development/desa/population/publications/data base/index.asp). [b] Based on these figures, the authors suggest 'a conservative world total of roughly 30 million victims' (15). [c] Based on these estimates, the authors suggest: 'It [total deaths] was of the order of 50 million. However, ... even this vast figure may be substantially lower than the real toll, perhaps as much as 100 percent understated' (105). [d] Total estimated deaths for 48 countries (which accounts for 80 per cent of the world population) extrapolated to the total world population. [e] Johnson and Muller (2002) data updated based on studies published during 1988–2020, which permitted increasing the geographical coverage to 72 countries. The total for the 72 countries (accounting for 94 per cent of the world population) is extrapolated to the world population.
Source: as noted on the table.

caveat that 'even this vast figure may be substantially lower than the real total, perhaps as much as 100 per cent understated' (105).

In this study we have updated estimates of Johnson and Muller (2002) based on a comprehensive survey of the studies published during 1998–2020 combined with data for some countries from hitherto unpublished official sources. Estimated total deaths in the 72 countries we have covered are between 32.5 million and 41.3 million. When extrapolated pro-rata to the total world population, the total global death toll is between 34.7 million and 44.0 million (Table 1). These numbers can possibly understate the true figure to the extent that the average death rate of countries not covered (in particular, countries in the Arab Middle East and some countries in Africa and Eastern Europe) exceeded the average global death rate used in the extrapolation.[13] However, after allowing for

---

[13] There is anecdotal evidence that some countries in the Middle East (e.g., Lebanon, Libya, and Iraq), which are not covered in our estimate, suffered significant influenza mortality through troop movement during the final year of WW1 (Gassem, 2020; Steinberg, 2002). Also, data are not available from Lusophone countries (Portuguese-speaking countries) and many francophone

such underestimation we believe that 100 million deaths, the figure suggested by Johnson and Muller (2002) as a possible upper bound and cited in some recent literature, is well off the mark.

If we take 50 million as a reasonable number, the number of total deaths of the 1918–20 pandemic is perhaps comparable to the other two mega pandemics in recorded human history, the Plague of Justinian around (540 AD) and the Black Death ((1347–50 AD) (Alfani & Murphy, 2017), that occurred during the pre-modern era. The death tolls of these two pandemics are estimated at around 25–50 million and over 50 million, respectively. The mortality rates of these two pandemics would also have been far greater given the low world population at those times. However, in terms of the number of deaths, the 1918–20 pandemic is by far the biggest in the modern history. The death toll of the other recorded pandemics during this period ranged from 400 thousand to 1.2 million (Fan et al., 2018).

A hallmark of the 1918–20 pandemic compared to other influenza pandemics before and after it is the high mortality rate. The seasonal flu is 'generally a mild, almost pleasurable experience, an opportunity for an unexpected fortnight's holiday from work' (Burnet, 1953: 276), with a mortality rate of only about 0.01 per cent (Taubenberger, 2003). By contrast the estimated median global mortality rate of the 1918–20 pandemic was about 2.3 per cent (Table 1). Why was the mortality rate so high?

The most ubiquitous explanation of tremendous morbidity and death rates relates to 'war conditions' encountered during the time of the pandemic. More than 70 million servicemen (both men in uniforms and military labourers ('Labour Corps')) were engaged in the war. These men came not only from the warring nations but also from their colonies and protectorates all over the world. The crowding of troops in war camps and ships, medical camps, and hospitals and the upheaval of normal life during wartime provided the best possible opportunity for the spread of airborne pathogens (Honigsbaum, 2020; Morens & Fauci, 2007; Wever & van Bergen, 2014). Close quarters far from help, such as ships on the high seas and war camps, were an ideal setting for the propagation of infectious disease. Massive troop movement across the seas was the main conduit of the global spread of the virus.

Some researchers in the field of evolutionary theory of virus postulate that the mutation of the 1918 virus into the more virulent form that caused the deadly second wave was a direct result of the unique conditions on the Western Front (Byerly, 2005; Ewald 1994, 2011; Roes, 2018; Woolhouse et al., 2002). In war

---

countries in Africa, which were presumably affected by the Africa-wide spread of the pandemic (Phillips, 2017).

camps and trenches where the pool of hosts remained packed with little mobility, there was less evolutionary pressure on the virus to moderate its virulence through *natural selection*.[14] Random genetic mutation could, in principle, produce a more lethal virus, but pathogens that are too lethal might not survive long enough to effectively transmit to different populations if the host is mobile. The mutated (second wave) virus, therefore, had the capacity to penetrate through the entire respiratory tract of the infected person and trigger a cytokine storm, which ravages the immune system (Tsoucalas et al., 2016; Viboud et al., 2013).

The 'war conditions' provided the setting for the propagation of the disease and perhaps the mutation of the virus into a deadly form, and the soldier movement facilitated the global transmission of the disease. However, the 1918–20 pandemic was not merely a 'war pandemic' (Jefferson & Ferroni, 2009: 1). Although the initial epicentre of the pandemic was the warring nations in Western Europe and North America, the pandemic gained its own momentum in the 'global periphery', the present-day developing countries,[15] most of which at the time were colonies of Western powers. As we will see in the next section, the pandemic mortality rate was almost four times higher in these countries, which accounted for over 90 per cent of the total estimated deaths. Malnutrition and comorbidity (concurrent prevalence of other diseases such as malaria, cholera, and tuberculosis (TB)) added to an individual's susceptibility to the virus. Near-famine conditions and food shortage made matters worse in India, Iran, and some other countries (Afkhami, 2003; Arnold, 2019; Liew, 2007; Mills, 1986).

Nineteenth-century movements to improve sanitation occurred simultaneously in several European countries and were built upon foundations laid in the period between 1750 and 1830. By the time of the pandemic, fundamental knowledge of sanitation, hygiene, and principles of disease transmission had become commonplace in public life in advanced economies in Europe and the United States. The knowledge of the mechanism of respiratory spread and means of preventing respiratory transmission had been accumulating since the beginning of the sanitation movement in the 1840s (Morens et al., 2021; Rosen, 2015). However, in the global periphery, the sanitary movement had begun to have some impact only in major cities. Colonial administrations generally did not have political will, administrative capacity, and the technical resources to introduce and administer sanitary practices (Wilson, 2016; Klein, 1973).

---

[14] Natural selection of a virus is its mechanism of evolution – the change in the heritable traits that shape its survival and spread.

[15] In the rest of the paper these countries are referred to as 'developing countries' (and the rest as 'developed countries') for brevity.

3.2 Morbidity and Case Mortality

The available estimates of morbidity and case mortality rates of the 1918–20 pandemic are summarised in Table 2. Almost one-third of the world population was infected with the virus, and of them, about 2.5 per cent succumbed to death. This mortality rate is at least 250 times as high as that of the other recorded influenza pandemics (Taubenberger & Morens, 2006). A hallmark of the pandemic was its high case mortality rate (Jefferson & Ferroni, 2009).

There are notable differences between developed countries and developing countries listed in the table both in terms of morbidity and case mortality, and the difference is much larger relating to the case mortality rate. This difference is consistent with the view that pandemic death is a lot more than just a 'one germ – one disease affair' (BMJ, 1919: 499). Factors, other than the virulence of the virus, mediated through poverty and deprivation seem to have played a vital part in determining the survival of the infected. The median case mortality rate in India was as high as 10 per cent compared to the global average of 2.5 per cent. Interestingly, both morbidity rate and the case mortality rate among the jail population in India during the pandemic were much lower compared to that of the general population. This striking difference was most likely because people in jail in India were generally better fed and were less likely to die from the disease because of the availability of medical care (Mills, 1986).

The only available evidence on pandemic morbidity and mortality by gender comes from a study conducted by the US Public Health Service in some 12 locations in the country after the second wave (Collins, 1931). The study finds little difference between the sexes with respect to the incidence of both mortality and morbidity. From about 10 to 35 years of age, the infection rates for females were slightly greater than the rate for males, but at other ages there were only small differences that were not statistically significant. This is of particular interest in view of the fact that at this time many of the young, adult males of the country were in the army, and those who were living at home, and included in the surveys, might have constituted a more or less selected group who were not in as good physical condition as those who had gone into the army (1926–27).

3.3 Patterns of Fatality

The age profile of usual (seasonal) influenza mortality depicts a U-shape pattern: victims, as a rule, are very young and very old, with a higher survival rate for those in between. This was also the pattern in the first wave of the 1918–20 pandemic. In the second and third waves, however, the pandemic resulted in a higher than expected mortality rate amongst young adults (Burnet & White, 1972; Collins, 1931; Gagnon et al., 2013; Viboud et al., 2013). Both infants and elderly

Table 2 Morbidity and case mortality during the 1918–20 influenza pandemic (%)

World/country	Source	Morbidity	Case mortality
World	Burnet and Clark (1942)	32.0	2.5
Australia	National Museum of Austrasia (undated)	40.0	0.7
USA	Frost (1920)[a]	28.0	1.6
British India[b]: general population	Tumbe (2020b)	40–60	10.0 <
British India:[b] jail population	Mill (1986), Table 1	33.7	4.4
Japan	Hayami (2015)	38.2	1.2
Korea	Lim (2011)	44.0	2.6
Nigeria	Ohadike (1991)	50.0–80.0	3.5–5.6
New Zealand	*Medical Journal of Australia* (1919)	33.0	1.2
The Philippines	Gealogo (2009)[c]	40.0	6.3
Thailand	Royal Thai Government (1919)	27.8	3.3

Note: [a] based on a survey of 130,000 people in 11 cities. [b] Includes Burma (Myanmar), Pakistan, and Bangladesh. [c] The data cover the second wave.
Source: as noted on the table.

did die in large numbers, but the great spike came in the middle: the death-age graph looked like a 'W' with the middle spike taller than the two sides. Two-thirds of the victims were adults aged between 20 and 40 years. This pattern was similar across the world. Also, the overall pattern was similar for both male and female victims, although the young adult peak of mortality was considerably higher among males than among females (Figure 1).

Burnet and Clark (1942: 90–9) came up with the postulate that the unusual 'W' shape age profile of second- and third-wave mortality can be explained in terms of the nature of the mutated virus and the way the body's defence mechanism changes with age. The mutated virus was of a very virulent strain that had the capacity to penetrate through the entire respiratory tract of all ages, and the young adults' bodies reacted so vigorously to the deadly virus that the reaction drowned them. A young adult has a peculiar ability to produce intense localised inflammatory response (not generalised) similar to the kind of reaction needed to deal with a localised injury such as broken bones, torn ligaments, and wounds.

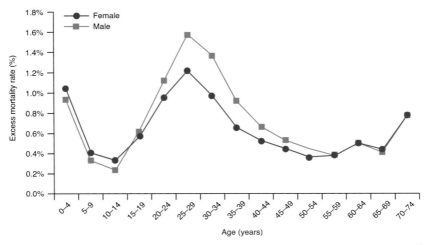

Figure 1 Median mortality by age and sex for the 1918–20 influenza pandemic[1]
Note: [1] based on data from 13 countries for which age-specific mortality data are available.
Source: Murray et al. (2006), Figure 1. Reproduced with permission.

When the stimulus is generated in 20–40-year-olds, as in the case of infection with the virulent flu virus, the intense inflammation in the lungs causes a springtide of fluids to overwhelm the lungs. After about 40 years of age, this ability to produce extreme inflammation declines, and the ability to survive generalised infection rises as the ability to survive localised injuries declines.

In Western countries the death rate amongst females was noticeably lower than that of males (Figure 1). However, the data for India revealed the reverse pattern in all age brackets: female mortality was higher (Chandra et al., 2012; Mills, 1986). It is postulated that this pattern is attributed to two innate societal factors: because of sex bias in family care, women were relatively more malnourished compared to men and hence less resistant to the flu virus,[16] and women had to bear the burden of taking care of the sick in the family. Interestingly, the Indian pattern of higher female mortality was also observed in Japan, but, in this case, only for the age brackets of 20 to 34 (Hayami, 2015). This presumably reflects greater involvement of women in this age group in household chores and greater susceptibility of pregnant women to viral infection (see Section 7.1).

According to data from the United States, the most vulnerable among the young adult females were pregnant women. The death rate amongst hospitalised pregnant women varied between 23 per cent and 71 per cent, and fetal death was

---

[16] This explanation is consistent with the phenomenon of 'missing women' (Sen, 1992).

encountered in over one-quarter (26 per cent) of pregnant women who survived (Barry, 2004a: 239). At the height of the second wave (September and October 1918), there was a 50 per cent increase in stillbirths in the United States (Jordan, 1927: 24). In India, the disease was particularly virulent for women of reproductive age (Chandra et al., 2012; Mills, 1986), and since the incidence of fatality was concentrated in the 20 to 40 age range, the pandemic left tens of thousands of widows and orphans in its wake (Arnold, 2019). Unlike in Western countries, in India mortality rates in rural areas far exceeded those of the cities (Davis, 1951; Wakimura, 1966).

4 Geography of Mortality

Notwithstanding the 'European' origin of the 1918–20 influenza pandemic, developing countries accounted for 86 per cent of the total estimated pandemic deaths of about 42 million[17] (Appendix, Figures 2 and 3). The median death rate of developing countries was 3.1 per cent compared to a global figure of 2.3 per cent and the developed-country average of about 1 per cent. There was a huge variation in the mortality rate among countries and geographical regions. Countries in Asia and Africa suffered the highest mortality rates – 3.0 per cent and 3.5 per cent, respectively. The death rate was much lower in Latin America (1.1 per cent) compared to Asia and Africa. Among all countries, the highest mortality rate was recorded in Western Samoa, where nearly one-quarter of the native population died, followed by Iran (14.5 per cent). In the Western countries, the death rate varied from 0.2 per cent to 1.5 per cent, with some European countries directly involved in the war recording rates at the upper end.

There was a heavy concentration of global pandemic deaths in British India, encompassing the present-day India, Pakistan, Bangladesh, and Myanmar (Burma).[18] The official estimate of total deaths that covered only the British-controlled provinces (which accounted for about 75 per cent of the population of British India at the time) was from 12 million to 14 million (Government of India, 1938). An Indian doctor who lived through the pandemic suggested a total of 15 million deaths (Sen, 1923). Davis (1951) estimated deaths by applying the excess death method to Decennial Census data between 18.5 and 22.6 million, concluding that a figure around 20 million (a death rate of 6.2 per cent) is as satisfactory as any. After adjusting Davis's estimate for possible overestimation bias, Mills (1986) came up with an estimate of 17–18 million.

---

[17] Median values of the reported lower- and upper-bound figures are used in the discussion in this section.

[18] Burma was governed by the British as part of India until 1937. Total population in Burma at the time was about 9 million (3 per cent of the total population of British India).

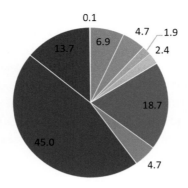

■ Africa (6.9 %)   ■ Middle East* (4.7%)

■ North America (1.9%)   ■ Latin america and the caribbean (2.4%)

■ East Asia (18.7%)   ■ Southeast Asia (4.7%)

■ South Asia** (45.0%)   ■ Europe (13.7%)

■ Oceania (0.1%)

Figure 2 Mortality of the 1918–20 influenza pandemic by world geographical regions (%)

Note: * Covers only Iran ** British India (includes present-day Myanmar, Pakistan, and Bangladesh) and Ceylon (Sri Lanka) (0.2 per cent)

Source: authors' illustration based on data from the Appendix.

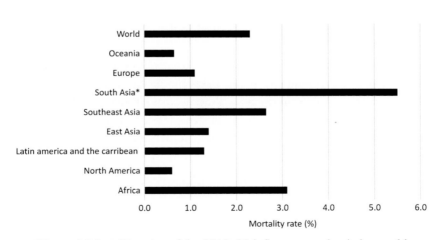

Figure 3 Mortality rates of the 1918–20 influenza pandemic by world geographical regions (%)

Note: * British India (includes present-day Myanmar, Pakistan, and Bangladesh) and Ceylon (Sri Lanka) (1.7 per cent).

Source: authors' illustration based on data from the Appendix.

Barro et al. (2020) estimated the death toll at 16.7 million. When estimated at the mid-point of Barro et al.'s and Davis's estimates, British India's mortality count (about 18 million) accounts for about 45 per cent of the total global pandemic deaths, with a mortality rate of 5.6 per cent.[19]

There was no centralised collection of vital statistics in China during this period. The estimates of 5–9 million given in the Appendix (from Patterson and Pyle 1991) are a guess based on the available data on pandemic death rates in neighbouring countries. These figures give a median death rate of 1.4 per cent, which is much lower than that of India (5.3 per cent) and even the global average (2.3 per cent). Iijima (2003), by applying mortality rates estimated from records of Chinese Maritime Customs in Chinese treaty ports, Hong Kong, Taiwan, and Kwangtung Leased Territory, came up with an even lower estimate of between 1 million and 1.28 million. Based on reports of foreign missionaries and information from the *China Medical Journal* (a journal edited by foreign experts), Jordan (1927) also observed that the influenza outbreaks in China 'were mild and did not spread widely'. Information put together from contemporary newspapers and administrative records of some large cities by Cheng & Leung (2007) and Langford (2005) suggest that the disease was widespread in China but was relatively mild and less lethargic than elsewhere in the world. According to Langford (2005), in Shanghai, the crude mortality rate was in fact lower in 1918 and 1919 than it was for any other year between 1913 and 1919. He observed a similar pattern in Hong Kong. In these two cities, the mortality rates were surprisingly lower than in other big cities like New York, London, and Bombay at the time. These studies provide three possible reasons for China's presumably relatively low incidence of pandemic death: effectiveness of traditional medicine, immunity gained by many people in China from previous influenza outbreaks (which had been a recurrent occurrence in the county), and limited mobility of people within inland China because of a poorly developed transport system.

Humphries (2014) argues the evidence of surprisingly low 1918–20 pandemic mortality in China is consistent with the view that the virus responsible for the 1918–20 pandemic in fact originated in China 4. When a population is exposed to a virus, those who survive develop a degree of immunity to subsequent outbreaks of the same (or similar) virus. 'If the flu originated in China, diffused around the globe, and returned the following year, this could explain

---

[19] Hill (2011) and Chandra et al. (2012) have estimated British India's excess death using province level and district level census data, respectively, and applying more refined estimation methods. However, their estimates, which range between 10.9 million and 13.9 million, do not cover the Indian Princely States and Burma.

why Langford found that flu mortality did not peak in Shanghai or Hong Kong' (Humphries, 2014: 71).

In Indonesia, vital statistics of Dutch administration relate almost exclusively to Java Island. Even for Java, data are difficult to analyse not only because of substantial underreporting of the number of deaths but also because of considerable confusion about the accuracy of the population base. Colonial records are virtually complete for the European population and probably nearly complete for the group classified as 'other foreigners' (almost entirely ethnic Chinese) but are deficient in coverage for the remainder of the population (Gardiner & Oey, 1987; Nitisastro, 1970). Brown (1987) estimates the death toll at 1.5 million. This was an informed guess based on administrative records and case studies (mostly qualitative) of some parts of the other islands. Chandra (2013) has estimated excess population lost during the pandemic at between 4.26 million and 4.37 million for the core island of Java, which accounts for about 90 per cent of the total Indonesian population. These figures, when applied to the total population of 37.9 million in Java, suggest a mortality rate of between 12 per cent and 13 per cent. This is unbelievably high compared to the mortality rate of India and the globalist rate of between 2.5 per cent and 5.0 per cent.

Van der Eng (2020) has illustrated that Chandra's methodology had resulted in overestimation of population loss because it was based on an overestimation of the growth rate (1.75 per cent) used for estimating the benchmarked growth rate for 1918. Based on a careful study of vital statistics from the village registers of the Dutch administration and with adjustments for underestimation of population numbers using data from the 1930 population census, van der Eng (2020) estimated a population growth date of 1.0 per cent to 1.1 per cent which is much more consistent with the existing body of knowledge on population dynamics in Indonesia during this period. By applying these alternative growth rates to Chandra's methodology, van der Eng has come up with a pandemic excess population loss figure of 1.47 million pandemic-related excess mortality in Java, and to 1.63 million for the whole country, when extrapolated on a pro-rata basis. The latter figure gives a death rate of 3.2 per cent, which is the second-highest in Asia after India.[20]

Countries in the Middle East, in particular Lebanon, Saudi Arabia, Persia (Iran) and Iraq, were directly exposed to the spread of the pandemic from the Western Fronts through troop movement during the final year of WW1 (Gassem, 2020; Steinberg, 2002). However, the available historiography of

---

[20] The extrapolation of the Java figure to the entire country was justified based on a major study undertaken in 1920 by a committee appointed by the public health administration of the colonial government to study the pandemic. According to this study, the incidence of pandemic death was roughly the same in the outer islands.

pandemic has so far covered only Iran (Afkhami, 2003). During the war, Iran had declared neutrality to all belligerent powers. However, given Iran's geographical centrality within the European plateau, Ottoman, Russian, and the British armies were fitting within its territory. Therefore, the pandemic invaded the country in 1918 through troop movements from several different directions. The country was very vulnerable to the pandemic because of widespread starvation caused by falling food production during summers in 1916 and 1917 and occupying armies' requisitioning of what food was left, high incidence of debilitating diseases such as malaria, cholera, anaemia, typhus, and other infectious deceases, as well as widespread popular addiction to opium. The estimated casualties were between 0.9 million and 2.4 million out of a total population of 11.2 million: a mortality rate of between 8.0 per cent and 21.7 per cent (Afkhami, 2003). This was the highest pandemic mortality rate for any country other than the unique case of Western Samoa. As in India, rural regions recorded the most casualties. The mortality rate in cities was in the range of 1 per cent to 10 per cent.

The coverage of African countries in the Appendix is dominated by those under the British administration. No data are available for all Lusophone Africa (i.e. Angola, Mozambique, Guinea Bissau, Cape Verde, Sao Tome, and Principe and Equatorial Guinea) and most Francophone African countries. According to a continent-wide overview of the pandemic, Phillips (2017) estimates the death toll at around 2.4 million (about 1.8 per cent of the continent's population at the time. The inter-country difference seems to reflect the combination of three features: exposure to the first wave that provided a cover against the impact of the virulent second wave, being part of the transport networks of the continent by sea or land, and being traversed by large number of people on the move, such as soldiers, sailors, and migrant workers. The worst affected countries were the ones where all three factors were present: South Africa, Kenya, Cameroon, Gold Coast (Ghana), Gambia, Tanganyika, and Nyasaland (Malaki). The other countries in the continent that were less exposed to the pandemic through troop movements or not linked with port cities through rivers and railroads (mostly the countries in northern and central Africa) were less affected (Gewald, 2007). A recent study (Rose, 2021) has estimated the death toll in Egypt between 138,000 and 170,000, about 1 per cent of the total population.[21] Egypt was important for the British military for mobilising human and natural resources for the war against the Ottoman Empire.

---

[21] The death toll in Egypt was lower presumably because a significant number of inhabitants had already gained immunity from the exposure to the mild first wave (through soldier movements) before the lethal second wave struck (Phillips, 2017).

Overall, there is a notable variation in the pandemic mortality rate across countries and continents. The array of reasons presented in various studies for this spatial variation includes pre-pandemic income levels and poverty, nutritional status, diurnal fluctuation in temperature, comorbidity, the timing of arrival of the virus, proximity to military bases and ports, and the use of non-pharmaceutical intervention (NPI). The nature of data availability does not permit systematic empirical analysis to delineate the impact of these proposed determinants. However, even a cursory eyeballing of the data reveals that the death toll was 'strongly mediated by per capita income levels' (Scheidel, 2017: 441). According to a simple bi-variate analysis undertaken by Murray et al. (2006) covering 27 countries, a 10 per cent increase in per capita income is associated with a 9 per cent to 10 per cent increase in the mortality rate. The sample of countries used in this calculation is dominated by advanced countries (with only seven of the present-day developing countries). The measured degree of relations would have been much stronger with a balanced sample of countries.

In a pioneering study of the natural history of infectious disease, Gill (1928) came up with the proposition that the amplitude of the diurnal range of temperature processes a special significance from the point of view of transmission (and hence the mortality rate) of the 1918–20 pandemic. This proposition was based on a study of the relationship between death rates of provinces with the amplitude of the diurnal range of temperatures in British India, with western, north-western, and central regions recording much higher mortality rates (Table 3).[22] The map he constructed revealed that mortality in different provinces of India did indeed bear some relationship to the average range of temperature in the peak month of mortality in India as a whole (Gill, 1928: 260). In particular, he noted that 25°F isogram not only divided high and low mortality areas but also divided clearly tropical from the sub-tropical parts of India (261).

Burnet and Clark (1942: 97) observe that Gill's conjecture is consistent with the possibility that Eastern provinces, with their lower humidity, and less fluctuation in temperature, might present less favourable conditions for the action of bacterial infection[23] and hence the death rate of infected people. Langford and Storey (1992: 111) note low temperature due to altitude may have played a role (in addition to the congested and unhygienic living conditions) in excessively higher pandemic mortality rates of Indian Tamils in the plantation sector in Sri Lanka compared to those in the rest of the country.

---

[22] As already noted, official figures used in this table understate the actual death rate. However, ordering of the rate across provinces is unlikely to have significantly affected by the overall degree of underestimation.

[23] 'The virus initiated the illness . . . , but when a fatal outcome resulted it was almost always the bacteria which were fully responsible' (Burnet & White, 1972: 122).

Table 3 Pandemic death rate in British India, 1918

Province	Death rate per thousand
Central Provinces and Berar	56.8
Delhi	55.6
Bombay	45.9
Punjab	42.2
North-West Frontier Province	40.0
United Province	22.9
Coorg	19.0
Madras	12.7
Assam	11.4
Bihar and Orissa	10.3
Burma	6.0
Bengal	4.7
British India	20.6

Source: Gill (1928).

Mills (1986) casts doubt on the validity of Gill's hypothesis. Using the province-level administrative records relating to the Indian jail population, which provide data on both morbidity and mortality, Mills demonstrates that the prevalence of influenza was fairly consistent across India and that what varied was the mortality rate. He, therefore, argues that the relationship found by Gill does, then, seem to correspond to the observed special variation in influenza mortality rate, rather than transmission (susceptibility to the virus), and hence understanding of the causal mechanism requires studying precise causes of the spatial differences in influenza mortality. He suggests that the role of malnutrition mainly caused by famine in North, West, and Central India may also help explain the geographical distribution of mortality within India. He further argues that the existence of the disease in climatically different countries/areas across the world is not consistent with the view that climatic conditions are relevant for explaining the pandemic's impact. To support the latter argument, he cites a comparative analysis of the impact of pandemic depths in the British empire undertaken by the Ministry of Health, UK (1920), according to which climate had little part to play on the world scale.

Reyes et al. (2018) examine the role of demographic factors, environmental variables, and mobility process within India on the versed patterns of pandemic mortality in India using data across 206 districts from January 1916 to December 1920. The study finds that population density and rainfall explained the spatial variation in excess mortality, and long-distance travel (mobility via rail roads) contributed to the observed spatial diffusion of the disease. However, they have stopped short of testing the Gill hypothesis, which is still relevant for understanding spatiotemporal pattern of pandemic deaths, even if there is no link between diurnal temperature and pandemic transmission. The relative importance of differences in diurnal temperature, comorbidity, food scarcity, and other related factors in determining spatial differences of susceptibility to influenza pandemics remains an unresolved issue.

5 Public Policy Response

Given the state of medical research and absence of a known medical antidote to influenza or its complications at the time, pharmaceutical intervention in the pandemic was limited only to general healthcare and nursing with some untested palliatives. One potentially effective therapy for reducing the risk of death was the use of convalescent sera collected from patients after their infection and administered to patients with current infection (Jester et al., 2018). As already noted, even general healthcare was largely available only in Western countries. The only recorded evidence of the use of vaccination during the pandemic comes from the United States, Japan, and Australia. At a time when the influenza virus was unknown and the medical profession's knowledge was confined only to associate bacteria, most of the vaccines used there were arbitrary mixtures of attenuated pneumococci, streptococci, and Pfeiffer's bacillus, pyogenes, and neisseria species

In the United States, numerous vaccines against the flu were developed and distributed, but in truth, they were at best placebos (Crosby, 2003: 100–104). In Japan, the government launched a nationwide vaccination campaign (Hayami, 2015). It is not known whether this had any effect on preventing secondary pneumonic infections. In Australia, Commonwealth Serum Laboratories (CSL) (set up during WW1) produced an experimental vaccine, a mixture of chemically killed bacteria to address secondary bacterial infections. Between 15 October 1918 and 15 March 1919, CSL issued three million doses for free distribution in Australia. Also, the Australian military used the vaccine in Samoa. Later evaluation found that the vaccine was effective in preventing death in inoculated individuals, presumably by preventing secondary bacterial infection (National Museum of Australia, undated; Shanks, 2018).

The overall high global death rate undoubtedly mirrored the state of clinical drug development at the time. There were no antidotes to influenza or secondary infection with bacteria. While the virus initiated the illness in every case, it was almost always a superimposed bacterial infection that was finally responsible for fatality. Given the unavailability of treatment for influenza or bacterial infection, the best the medical profession could do was prescribe palliatives or provide patients with supportive care to facilitate natural recovery.

While the poor state of clinical drug development was obviously responsible for high death rates in all countries, there was a vast gap in the provision of institutionalised healthcare between Western countries and developing countries. As has been well documented, imperial powers paid little attention to public health in their colonies (Arnold, 2019; Balfour & Scott, 1924; Killingray, 2003; Patterson and Pyle, 1983; Tomkins, 1994; Wibowo et al., 2009). Whatever available healthcare facilities were confined mostly to large cities. Even in cities, health workers due to their limited knowledge resorted to treatments based on trial and error. For instance, in Indonesia quinine and opium were used as alternative medicines (Wibowo, 2009). In rural areas, where the majority of people lived, infected people and families had to fend for themselves. Most people turned to traditional medicine or folk remedies and practices. In the absence of public healthcare and a social safety net, the rate of mortality was increased by 'innate susceptibility' and a lack of care when all members of a family were incapacitated. In India, many officers of the Indian Medical Service had been drafted into war service overseas (Arnold 2019; Phillips, 2017). In African countries, people even shunned available facilities and palliatives because of the anti-colonial mentality and their belief in the failure of Western medicine. The European origin of the disease and the failure of European medicine to effectively treat the virus gave rise to an influential anti-colonial campaign in most African countries that had a significant lingering impact on public health in these countries well beyond the pandemic years (Arnold, 1988; Ohadike, 1991; Phillips, 2017).

The available evidence on 'non-pharmaceutical interventions' (NPIs) during the pandemic comes mostly from studies conducted in the United States. Crosby (2003) provides a comprehensive state-by-state study of social distancing measures in the United States: closure of schools, theatres, and places of worship, restrictions on mass gatherings, quarantines at port and railway stations, and public information campaigns. According to his findings, New York was less affected than other East Coast metropolises because of a solid foundation in public health and administrative experience gained from its 30-year war on TB. Philadelphia (East Coast) had the most severe experience of any major American city whilst San Francisco suffered the most amongst West Coast cities. The measures introduced early and kept in place after the danger had passed played an important role. Based on an interstate comparative analysis of the nature and effectiveness of NPIs, Crosby came up with the general inference that the demands of national security, a thriving economy, and public health are rarely aligned, and elected representatives defending the first two undermine the third.

In a comparative analysis of NPIs implemented in two cities in Minnesota, Ott et al. (2007) find that St. Paul had a much higher case fatality rate compared with Minneapolis presumably because St. Paul chose to strictly implement self-isolation and Minneapolis did not. Individuals with influenza who had their status reported in St. Paul had to endure isolation until they were released with a physician's approval. This seems to have had the unintended consequence of discouraging people from seeking the attention of physicians. In contrast, in Minneapolis, given the absence of enforced isolation, more people might have felt comfortable seeking medical attention.

According to the findings of Bootsma and Ferguson (2007), time-limited interventions of social distancing reduced total mortality only moderately (perhaps 10–30 per cent), and the impact was often limited because interventions were introduced too late and/or lifted too early. Even in the absence of government intervention, individuals spontaneously reduced their contact rates in response to high levels of mortality during the pandemic. If interventions were very effective at containing the virus at an early stage, the likelihood of a second peak in mortality at a subsequent wave could have been higher because there was a larger number of susceptible people in the population who had not been previously exposed to the virus.

Markel et al. (2007) estimate the impact of school closures, prohibition of public gatherings, and quarantine isolation in 43 US cities during the second wave of the pandemic (September 1918–February 1919). The results suggest that the impact of these NPIs in determining city-to-city variation in mortality was associated with both the timing and duration of implementation. The cities that implemented the NPIs promptly had significant delay in reaching peak mortality and lower the peak and total mortality rates. At the same time, there was a statistically significant positive association between the duration of NPIs and the total mortality rate. Barro (2020) questions the validity of the 'exogeneity' assumption underlying this analysis: NPIs, measured by the length of time in force, are determined by city governments independently of the pandemic-related death rate. Barro (2020) contends that the City governments are likely to determine the length of NPIs in response to the death rates. He accounts for the potential endogeneity bias by estimating the relationship by using distance from Boston to each city as an instrumental variable for NPIs.[24] The alternative findings confirm that NPIs clearly help reducing the peak mortality to the level of average mortality rate ('flattening the curve'), but the estimated effect of NPIs on

---

[24] The second wave of the pandemic in the US first began around Boston in August 1918 with the returning of troops from Europe and then spread to the rest of the country. Barro (2020) therefore consider that distance from Boston serve as an exogenous measure of how early the pandemic reach each city in the sample.

overall mortality rate is small and statistically insignificant. The upshot is that NPIs delay deaths but do not ultimately avoid them over time. However, flattening the curve itself can be considered a significant gain from NPIs because it could ease burden on the health system, possibly leading thereby to fewer deaths.

The experiences of countries in Oceania, in particular the difference between Australia and New Zealand relating to pandemic mortality, figure prominently in discussions on the effectiveness of quarantine measures during the pandemic (Burnet & Cark, 1942; Johnson, 2006). Both Australia and New Zealand had the advantage of being 'island' nations situated far away from the epicentre of the pandemic. However, the death rate of New Zealand turned out to be much higher than that of Australia. The virus reached both countries in August 1918 at the end of the first wave. Australia immediately responded with strict maritime quarantine in all ports. The one-week quarantine requirement was applicable to both incoming and outgoing vessels. Thanks to these measures, Australia was not affected by the deadly second wave of the pandemic, and the country celebrated the armistice in November having nothing to fear from the virus. *The Medical Journal of Australia* (1919) reported that 'the Federal Quarantine Service will be in the proud position of having achieved the greatest triumph of its kind in the history of epidemiology'. However, Australia was affected by the third wave after the quarantine requirements were relaxed in early January. New Zealand, where there was no systematic quarantine (and/or social distancing requirements), was affected by both the second and third waves (Rice, 1988, 2003). The overall pandemic death rate in New Zealand was 0.65 per cent compared to 0.3 per cent in Australia. Australia's death rate was one of the lowest recorded in any country during the pandemic (Appendix).

Australia's strict quarantine measures applied equally to outgoing vessels from the Australian ports. As a result pacific islands exclusively served by Australian ships (the Gilbert and Ellice groups, the New Hebrides, and Norfolk and Solomon Islands) were also saved by the worst ravages of the pandemic (McQueen, 1976). By contrast, the death rates in the island nations served by the regular shipping service (*Talune*) from Auckland (Western Samoa, Fiji, Tonga, and Nauru) were much higher (Burnet & Clark, 1942: 14). American Samoa escaped infection because of strict quarantine imposed by the US naval administration (Tomkins, 1992).

According to the limited available evidence for African counties, NPIs had little impact on preventing the spread of the disease (Andayi et al., 2019; Ohadik, 1991; Patterson 1983; Phillips 2017; Ranger, 1992; Sambala 2012). The colonial governments did little to inform the population about the pandemic or to give advice on how to take care of the infected. Quarantine measures at entry points were mostly ineffective. In Gold Coast (Ghana), officials in Accra were of the view that 'quarantine measures were useless and needlessly disruptive and should not be attempted' (Patterson, 1983: 210). Restrictions on gathering and school closures were limited to only cities and urban areas. There was no targeted income support or other relief measures and people were left to fend for themselves, especially in rural areas.

A key theme of the historiography of the 1918–20 pandemic in British India is that the absence of a well-organised administrative machinery for governing public health and the poor quality of sanitary infrastructure significantly contributed to the severity of the ravage compared to the rest of the world (Arnold, 2019, 2020; Klein, 1973; Phipson, 1923; Sen, 1923). This, in turn, is considered a reflection of the colonial government's failure to learn from the past natural disasters and outbreaks of infectious diseases in the country. Throughout the British period (and of course prior to that), India experienced extraordinarily high rates of mortality caused by famines and recurrent bouts of cholera, plague, smallpox, and malaria (Klein, 1973). In 1896, a bubonic plague that began in 1896 and lasted for two decades caused some 12 million deaths (Arnold, 2019). However, there was no significant initiative on the part of the colonial administration to develop administrative capacity and technical resources to face such calamities in the future. British India was therefore caught off guard by the onset of the pandemic.

The recent study by Sekher (2021) of the experience of the Princely State of Mysore provides an interesting counterpoint for understanding the government failure in British India at large in managing the pandemic. For reasons not still well understood, Mysore was widely considered a 'progressive princely state' with administrative modernisation, state support for social services – mainly for education and health – and the introduction of representative institutions throughout the British period (Ramusack, 2004). The pandemic morbidity and mortality rate (15.5 per cent and 2.9 per cent, respectively) were less than half of that of the entire British India (Table 2). Based on a penetrating study of archival record, Sekher (2021: 37) infers that the well-organised administrative machinery and health and sanitary infrastructure made it possible for Mysore to minimise the calamity. The key elements of its strategy of combatting the pandemic included 'a combination of strong administrative measures, including strict monitoring of public health and sanitation services, timely gathering of data and information, well-organised relief operations, regulating the price of food grains, the administration's sensitivity towards public grievances and cultural sentiments, and the involvement of civilian and community organisations' (Sekher, 2021: 37).

6 Socio-economic Impact

For epidemiologists the 1918–20 pandemic served as a call to arms, giving rise to the era of virology.[25] For a researcher in this area of study, the major preoccupation in the next 14 years was to isolate the causes of influenza and thereby develop means of fighting against it (Burnet, 1953; Burnet & Clark, 1942). Prior to the pandemic, influenza was always referred to in the medical profession in a flippant fashion, as it presented a sharp contrast to the other prevailing infections (smallpox, typhus, typhoid fever, and the like) in terms of much lower mortality threat. There was also much confusion as to whether it was a viral or a bacterial disease, and since the virus was unknown only the associated bacteria could be studied.

By the early 1930s, there was an understanding that there was a virus responsible for influenza, which was different from that which caused the common cold. The influenza virus was discovered in 1933 by three British medical researchers, Wilson Smith, Christopher Andrews, and Patrick Laidlaw. This breakthrough paved the way to develop treatments to combat the illness. Discovery of penicillin, sulphonamides, and other potential antibiotics helped treat superimposed bacterial infection.

An important development in the mathematical theory of epidemiology that helped understand the spread of infectious diseases around this time was the SIR epidemiological model put forward by Kermack and McKendrik (1927). It broadened the understanding of the interplay of the number of susceptible individuals (S), the number of infected individuals (I), and the number recovered (R) in determining the spread of contagious epidemics/pandemics. This contribution to the mathematical theory of epidemics is extensively used by economists and health administrators in the current COVID-19 pandemic.

When the influenza virus was discovered in 1933, it was expected that the isolation of the aetiological agents would lead to speedy evaluation of prophylactic measures for the prevention of another disaster. However, this task proved to be more complex than was expected because tools to study its genome sequence (structure) were still in their infancy (Bernet & Clark, 1942). It was four decades later (1996–2005) that the viral gene was fully sequenced from ribonucleic acid (RNA) fragments of the 1918 pandemic virus and the latter was reconstructed as a fully infectious virus and studied experimentally by a team of US epidemiologists (Anne Reid, T. G. Fanning, John Hultin, J. Taubenberger, Pater Palese, and Adolfor Garcia-Sastre) (Jordan, 2020; Taubenberger et al., 2007). Subsequent research revealed that viral decedents of the 1918 'founder

---

[25] In the first comprehensive literature survey of influenza, Burnet and Clark (1942) covered 132 works, of which 95 per cent had been undertaken after 1918.

virus' are still circulating today as seasonal influenza A viruses, and subsequent pandemics in 1957, 1968, and 2009 were all caused by genetic updating of the 1918 virus (Taubenberger & Morens, 2020). This groundbreaking research, which took more than 15 years, helped the global public health community to prepare for future pandemic threats. Thanks to these medical advances, the complete genome sequences of SARS-COV-2 were made public in early January 2020 in less than a month after reporting of the first infection; by mid-2020 tens of thousands of genome sequences have already been published.

The advances in medical research propelled by the 1918–20 pandemic have set the stage for the development of medicine and preventative vaccines for influenza and other respiratory diseases. In particular, strong and consistent evidence on the interaction between influenza and secondary bacterial respiratory pathogens has helped develop prevention and treatment measures specifically related to bacterial infections that occur secondary to influenza. In addition to these medical advances, the traumatic experience of the pandemic has had a significant impact on public healthcare reforms in the sphere of healthcare. The 1920s saw many governments in Western countries embracing the concept of socialised healthcare and improvement in health data reporting systems with an emphasis on epidemic preparedness. These important developments are beyond the scope of this paper.[26] In this section, our sole focus is on the socio-economic effects of the pandemic.

6.1 Population Dynamics and Human Capital Development

The pandemic, given its unprecedented morbidity and mortality rates with devastating impact on most fertile and productive population cohorts, must have had significant consequences on demographic dynamics and human capital development that extended well beyond the pandemic years. However, in the Western countries that were directly involved in the war it is extremely difficult to separate out the demographic effects of the pandemic from those of the Great War (Johnson, 2006). Therefore, the available evidence on demographic effects of the pandemic comes largely from other countries that were not directly involved in the war.

In Norway, a climate of fear and uncertainty in 1918, alongside social distancing efforts and the peculiarities of Norwegian marriage laws (which imposed a one-year waiting period before widows could remarry), led to a drop in births in 1919, as families deferred childbearing (Mamelund, 2004). Higher rates of maternal mortality and miscarriage during the pandemic likely

---

[26] These developments have been well documented (see Burnet, 1979; Crosby, 2003: Chapter 13; Spinney, 2017: Chapter 19).

also contributed to a drop in birth rates. The pent-up demand for children (alongside 'replacement' demand for children lost to the pandemic) was activated after the crisis passed, resulting in a baby boom in 1920. Overall, Norway experienced a significant reduction in fertility rate during the pandemic, but the fertility rate recovered within about two years, reaching higher levels compared to the pre-pandemic years.

Changes in fertility following the pandemic arose from the way that pandemic mortality affected patterns of marriage. In Sweden, Boberg-Fazli et al. (2021) find evidence of a drop in fertility during the pandemic, followed by a short-lived rebound in post-pandemic fertility. The net effect in the long term, however, was to reduce fertility. This was due in part to persistent disruptions to marriage markets (particularly in rural areas and poorer cities); the adverse effects on income; as well as to behavioural changes induced by the pandemic, including a rise in female labour supply (and so, an increase in the opportunity cost of childrearing) in regions with high male pandemic mortality rates. Perhaps most noteworthy, the short-run post-pandemic fertility increase was selective in nature: a child born during the post-pandemic boom was more likely born to mothers of higher socio-economic status. This was largely driven by postponement of fertility, and particularly, selective postponement reflecting the effect of the pandemic on survivors' incomes.

Chandra et al. (2018) examine short-term birth sequelae of the pandemic using monthly data on births and all causes of death for 19 US states. Notable findings include (1) a drop in births in the 3 months following peak mortality, presumably due to increase in the rate of miscarriage and preterm delivery rate during the peak of the pandemic; (2) a steep drop in births occurring 9–10 months after the peak due to impaired conception, possibly due to effects on fertility and behavioural changes during the pandemic; and (3) a reversion in births to normal levels occurring 5–7 months after peak mortality.

In a study of the state of Sao Paulo state in Brazil, Guimbeau et al. (2020) found a rather larger reduction in sex ratios at birth following the 1918 influenza pandemic. This finding is consistent with the greater vulnerability of male fetuses to adverse *in utero events*, a phenomenon often seen in famines and environmental disasters. Such changes in the sex ratio, or in sex-specific survival, may well have had long-run implications for marriage and fertility.

Chandra and Yu (2015a, 2015b) examine pandemic-associated mortality and subsequent demographic dynamics in Taiwan and Japan. In both countries, there was a significant reduction in births after the pandemic mortality peaked in 1919, primarily through the mechanism of reduced conception and embryonic losses during the first month of pregnancy. In India, the age and sex selection effect of the pandemic, a combination of concentration of fatality in prime ages and the greater fatality rate among women, resulted in a decline in the birth rate in 1919 of around 30 per cent (Mills, 1986). However, there was a population spurt during the ensuing years of the interwar period, presumably because the spike in mortality during the pandemic left a diminished but healthier population (Klein, 1973, 1988). It seems that, as in India, the pandemic created a healthier population that was able to reproduce at a higher rate by pruning the less fit.

What are the long-term implications of the pandemic for the quality of the labour force over and above the direct impact on population dynamics? Almond (2006) addresses this issue by testing the 'fetal origin' hypothesis proposed by Barker (1992). This hypothesis postulates that disturbances that occur during key periods of fetal development can generate a wide range of latent effects leading to chronic health conditions and worse cognitive performance, which together have an adverse impact on health conditions, human capital accumulation and socio-economic status in adulthood.

Almond's test involved comparing human-capital traits and labour market performance of a cohort in utero during the height of the pandemic and a cohort in utero prior to the pandemic using Decennial Census data for the period 1960–80. The test was conducted using a unique data set compiled by combining the US 1960–80 census microdata and data on maternal and health conditions provided by US Vital Statistics. The findings suggest that the former cohort was characterised by lower educational attainment, increased rates of physical disability, accelerated adult mortality, lower income, greater dependence on higher transfer payments, and lower socio-economic status compared with those in the latter cohort. In addition, the results indicate that persons born in states with more severe exposure to the pandemic experienced worse outcomes than those born in states with less severe pandemic exposures.

Because of the absence of data on specific health outcomes in the Censuses, Almond was not able to identify physiologic pathways through which the disturbance that occur during fetal development impact on the quality of life in adulthood. Almond and Mazumdar (2005) fill this gap by using data from the US Survey of Income and Program Participation (SIPP). The findings indicate that the 1919 birth cohort, in particular, those born in the second quarter of 1919, who were in utero at the height of the pandemic, are 10 per cent more likely to report poor health than their counterparts born in surrounding years, with 17–35 per cent increase in a range of functional limitations, including trouble hearing, speaking, lifting, and walking; and are also likelier to experience diabetes and stroke. Moreover, these patterns manifest 65–80 years after the pandemic, suggesting that changes to fetal health can have life-long effects.

A number of subsequent studies cast doubt on the representativeness of the cohort of parents used in Almond's study to warrant treating the findings purely as biological consequences of in utero exposure to the pandemic.[27] The main contention was that, given that the pandemic coincided with the height of the WW1 enlistment, the 1919 birth cohort was more likely to be born into households with lower socio-economic status. Others debated the possibility of pandemic-induced self-selection in fertility.

Beach et al. (2018) reassessed whether parental selection is a compounder of Almond's findings by using a new data set that permitted controlling for observable parental characteristics. The results suggest that parental characteristics indeed attenuate results, but there is still strong evidence supporting Almond's inference that in utero exposure to the pandemic had lasting effects on human capital accumulation. Cook et al. (2019) add a new dimension to the 'fetal origin' literature by exploring the possibility of intergenerational persistence of these effects. They find evidence of multigenerational effects on educational attainment, occupational prestige, and family socio-economic status up to the third generation, the grandchildren of those exposed to the pandemic in utero. More specifically, they find a reduction of approximately one-tenth of a year of schooling for the first generation, one-fifth of a year of schooling for the second generation, and one-sixth of a year of schooling for the third generation, with relatively large effects on economic as well as health outcomes for the second generation.

A number of subsequent studies have tested Almond hypothesis in a wider global setting while focussing on different channels through which the in utero effect impacts the quality of life in adulthood. In Taiwan, there is evidence of permanent scarring: cohorts exposed to the pandemic in utero faced penalties with respect to educational attainment, heights, kidney disease, circulatory and respiratory issues, and diabetes (Lin & Liu, 2014). Taiwan was a low-income country with minimal public health intervention at the time. A comparison of the finding with that of the United States suggests that even higher income levels of households failed to act as a buffer against the adverse effect.

Ogasawara (2018) estimates the lingering effects of fetal exposure to the 1918 influenza pandemic on the development of secondary school and girls' high school students in industrialising Japan. The study finds that fetal exposure to influenza in the pandemic years reduced the heights of boys and girls by approximately 0.28 cm and 0.14 cm, respectively – magnitudes which in other studies have been associated with substantial increases in the probability of type

---

[27] See Beach et al. (2020) and Almond and Currie (2011) for a comprehensive survey of the related literature.

II diabetes, osteoarthritis, and heart disease. Percoco (2016) finds that in Italy the cohort born during 1918–20 on average experienced a reduction of schooling by 0.3–0.4 years. However, this study does not specifically focus on in utero exposure to the pandemic. Nelson (2010), using data extracted from a country-wide labour market survey conducted in Brazil, finds that those who were in utero during the pandemic are less likely to have formal education and be college educated, have formal employment, and are engaged in pursuits with lower hourly wages compared to individuals born in the few years surrounding the Influenza Pandemic. These findings are corroborated by the results reported in Guimbeau et al. (2020) for Sao Palo. Neelsen and Stratmann (2012) specifically explore possible sex differences in the in utero effect. Using data from the 1970 Swiss census, they find that the male cohort that had fetal exposure to the pandemic performed significantly worse compared to their female counterparts in terms of educational attainment and had a lower chance of marriage than those belonging to the surrounding cohorts. The finding relating to these later-life outcomes is remarkably robust to interregional differences in influenza severity. A study in Sweden has come up with mixed findings (Helgertz & Bengtsson, 2019). Both men and women with fetal exposure in the pandemic experienced higher morbidity at ages 54–87. For males, exposure during the second trimester was also associated with cancer and heart disease. However, the study failed to provide consistent evidence supporting any long-term consequences of fetal exposure relating to adulthood income, social status, and occupational attainment.

Fletcher (2018) uses data from the 1960 US Decennial Census to examine whether individuals exposed in utero to the 1918/19 influenza pandemic had different family formation patterns than adjacent unexposed cohorts. The findings suggest small overall effects on marriage rates, number of children, and several measures of 'type' of spouse for men, but moderate effects for women. For example, women with in utero exposure during their first trimester marry men with 0.2 fewer years of schooling than those not exposed. There is also evidence that exposed individuals have spouses with lower schooling than unexposed counterparts, this effect is particularly large for women, and it increases the likelihood of marrying spouses with very low levels of schooling.

An important impact on economic well-being of the surviving population of a pandemic pertains to temporal and cross-disease mortality spillover resulting from pandemic-era mortality patterns. In a rare study of this phenomenon, Noymer (2011) shows that the 1918 influenza pandemic hastened the decline of tuberculosis in the US through a 'harvesting' mechanism, driven by substantial age overlap in the profile of prospective tuberculosis and (pandemic-type) influenza victims. This harvesting, in turn, had important long-lived implications for sex differences in post-pandemic mortality rates in favour of males. This was because tuberculosis morbidity disproportionately affects men, and the influenza pandemic reduced the pool of those who might die of tuberculosis in the post-pandemic era.

Myrskylä et al. (2013) analyse how early exposure to the 1918 influenza pandemic is associated with old-age mortality by cause of death in the United States. The study finds a statistically significant trade-off between non-cancer and cancer causes: cohorts with high non-cancer mortality had low cancer mortality, and vice versa. Early disease exposure increases old-age mortality through non-cancer causes, which include respiratory and cardiovascular disease, and may trigger a trade-off in the risk of cancer and noncancerous causes. Potential mechanisms include inflammation or apoptosis. Adverse early life conditions may have lasting effects on old-age health and mortality.

Finally, in an agrarian society, the pandemic death toll can have long-term effects on demographic dynamics and human capital through income/wealth effect on the survived population, as Donaldson and Keniston (2016) have found in a study of India. The 1918 influenza pandemic struck India when the subcontinent was mired in its long-term Malthusian equilibrium of low population growth and stable per-capita consumption. Its terrible death toll left survivors with additional agricultural land, which was rapidly put to agricultural use with no decrease in yields. This increased per-capita wealth gave rise, over the ensuing decades, to heightened investments in both child quantity as well as child quality: families in districts with a high pandemic death toll had more children in the aftermath of influenza. These children were taller and better educated.

6.2 Economic Performance

Barro et al. (2020) undertake a multi-country (42 countries) panel data analysis of the impact of pandemic deaths on economic growth and private consumption, after controlling for WW1 deaths. The results suggest that the pandemic mortality was associated, on average, with a reduction in real per capita GDP by 6 per cent and real private consumption by 8 per cent, and a 20 percentage point increase in the inflation rate. The contraction in economic growth and consumption was accompanied by a substantial short-term decline in real return financial assets (measured by returns on stocks and government bonds), but there was no evidence of statistically significant impact on long-term return on these assets. These results need to be treated with caution because a number of countries in the sample were directly involved in the WW1: the number of combat fatalities used as the control variable to net out the impact of the pandemic does not presumably capture the full economic effect of the war on these countries. Moreover, the annual data used in the analysis do not appropriately capture the direct impact of the pandemic which was heavily concentrated in the last two quarters of 1918 and the first quarter of 1919 in most countries.

Velde (2020) examines the impact of the pandemic on the US economy using high-frequency data. The analysis focuses on industrial production stock market volatility. The results indicate that industrial production contracted by about 20 per cent in the fourth quarter of 1918 driven by labour shortages but recovered swiftly (an 'exceptionally brief' V-shape recovery); the Armistice possibly prolonged the 1918 recession, short as it was, by injecting momentary uncertainty. There is also evidence that the US and the UK stock markets were remarkably resilient to the pandemic shock. These findings are consistent with contemporary reports of the economy by the US Federal Reserve Bank and business cycle literature encompassing the pandemic period (Burns & Mitchell, 1946; Ogburn & Thomas, 1922). However, it is risky to generalise from the US experience. The United States joined the war in its final year and it experienced an economic boom during the first three years fuelled by war demand. The boom dissipated as the war ended. Moreover, production bases in the United States were not affected unlike those in the warring nations in Europe.

Velde's (2020) interpretation of the labour market effects that underpinned industrial recession is consistent with the findings of Garrett (2009). This comparative study of the impact of mortalities of the 1918–20 pandemic and WW1 on wage growth in the US manufacturing sector indicates that the states and cities that experienced greater influenza mortalities experienced higher wage growth relative to the states and cities that experienced greater war casualties.

Jordà et al. (2022) examine medium- to long-term impacts of return on assets of the 1918–20 influenza pandemic and 18 other disasters (both wars and pandemics, each of which accounted for at least 100,000 deaths) using a data set dating back to the fourteenth century and covering six countries (France, UK, Germany, Italy, Netherlands, and Spain). Real return on assets is measured in terms of real rates of interest on long-term debt. The results indicate that pandemics significantly depressed real asset return, and this impact lingers on for about four decades. Labour scarcity resulting from pandemic mortality and morbidity that drive up real wages relative to the cost of capital and reshuffling of household asset portfolios towards greater precautionary savings are identified as underlying causes. Interestingly, the comparative analysis of the study reveals a contrasting *positive* effect of wars on asset returns, presumably because capital is destroyed in wars (resulting in an increase in the relative cost of capital in post-war recovery) but not during a pandemic. A major limitation of the study is that the econometric analysis has lumped together all pandemics regardless of significant differences in their durations, which is a key determinant of long-term impact on economic performance. As already noted, an important feature of the 1918–20 pandemic was its exceptional brevity and moderate amplitude, which presumable would have significantly conditioned its long-term impact.

Brainerd and Siegler (2003) undertook an econometric analysis of post-pandemic growth in the United States using state-level data. The study found that the growth rate is *positively* associated with the death rate, possibly reflecting the capacity of a society to bounce back after a violent shock and/or weaker people could have been purged by the flu. However, this study has failed to separate the impact of the pandemic from effects of WW1. The above-average influenza deaths among prime-age adults were associated with above-average business failure in 1919 and 2920, but paradoxically, the pandemic was positively correlated with subsequent economic growth in 2020. Peace divi-dends of ending the war – reallocation of resources locked in the war effort and demobilisation of the armed forces – could have significantly contributed to stronger growth (Asquith, 2020).

Carillo and Jappelli (2020) examine the impact of the pandemic on Italy using region-leave annual data with WW1 death as a control variables. The results suggest a 6.5 per cent decline in GDP on average, with the impact dissipating within three years. The pandemic shock was associated with only a 0.8 per cent decline in the manufacturing share of total employment, presumably because at the time Italy was predominantly a rural economy with nearly 60 per cent of the labour force engaged in agriculture. Karlsson et al. (2014) and Dahl et al. (2020), respectively, provide evidence on the impact of the pandemic on neighbouring Sweden and Denmark, which were not involved in WW1 and where the pandemic death rate was also much lower (Appendix). In Sweden, there was no statistically significant effect on national income either during or after the pandemic, but in Denmark, there was a significant decline in return on capital accompanied by increase in real wages.

At the time of the 1918–20 pandemic, the present-day developing countries were predominantly agrarian economies. An interesting issue relating to the impact of the pandemic on these countries is therefore how labour shortages impacted agricultural production. Schultz (1964) probed this issue using data for Indian agriculture before and after the pandemic. This study was essentially a test of the theory of surplus labour of Arthur Lewis (1954), which was at the heart of development economics in the immediate post-war decades. The theory postulates that the agrarian economy of the typical developing country is characterised by a massive pool of surplus labour, and hence, marginal productivity of labour is zero. Therefore, this part of the labour force is wholly redundant and is available for industrialisation and other activities in the modern sector at no opportunity costs except the cost of transfer. Schultz (1964) considered Indian agriculture during the pandemic as an ideal case study of the surplus labour theory because the pandemic did not affect animals and other factors of production except for the number of workers, and the mortality rate in rural areas during the pandemic far exceeded that of urban areas.

The test involved a comparison of deaths attributable to the pandemic and change in acreage sown to crops in 10 provinces between 1916–17 and 1919–20. The results suggest that the reduction in the agricultural labour force by about eight per cent as a consequence of the pandemic was associated with a sharp reduction in acreage allocated to crops from 265 million in 1916–17 to 228 million in 1918–19 (Schultz, 1964: 66–7). He therefore concluded, 'It would be hard to find any support in these data for the doctoring that a part of the labour force in agriculture in India at the time of the epidemic had a marginal productivity to zero' (67).

In a critique of Schultz (1964), Sen (1967) argues that Schultz's test is inconclusive for two reasons. First, the concept of surplus labour assumes a pattern of family-wise labour withdrawal in response to some economic incentives. For example, migration to wage employment outside that withdrawal of labour force from the rural economy will keep the total output unchanged, whereas the influenza pandemic was not only unevenly distributed over families within a given region, it was unevenly distributed between different regions in a given province. Second, he cast doubt on the relevance of Schultz's findings for understanding the impact of the pandemic on the agricultural economy of India. The post-pandemic observations of Schultz's analysis were in 1919–20, which was the year immediately following the havoc, so there was little time allowed for the market to achieve the necessary allocation of land or labour, even if such a market worked well. Quoting data from the Census of India in 1921, Sen noted that the pandemic was not even over in the year of the observation.

The findings of Donaldson and Keniston (2016) on labour market effects on agricultural production in India are also supportive of the surplus labour hypothesis: the terrible death toll left survivors with additional agricultural land, which was put rapidly to agricultural use with no decrease in yields. A district-level study of the impact of the pandemic on women's labour market participation in India finds districts most adversely affected by influenza mortality saw a temporary increase in female labour force participation (the negative labour supply shock was counterbalanced by 'distress' labour supply by widows).

Brown (1987) has reported evidence, which is consistent with that of Sen, relating to the impact of pandemic mortality on agricultural production in Java and Madura in Indonesia. In 1919, the area under paddy and other smallholder crops in Java was generally higher than in 1917, thereby continuing the upwards trend established in the years immediately preceding the pandemic. Why did labour shortages not result in a contraction in the area under cultivation as Schultz observed in India? Brown alludes to two possible reasons: the agricultural sector had surplus labour (characterised by zero marginal productivity of labour) and/or the diminished labour supply in agriculture was supplemented by workers moving to agriculture from other sectors of the economy. A recent study on food production in Java during the pandemic provides evidence on the latter possibility (Gallardo-Albarrán & de Zwart, 2021). The mortality impact of influenza on Java was high: the crude mortality rates doubled in 1918 relative to the preceding years. However, aggregate food production did not decline because agricultural labour and land moved from sugar cultivation to food production in order to avoid famine. Those regions that were highly suitable for rice production saw a larger reduction in sugar production, and regions that had more flexible land tenure arrangements experienced substantially greater reductions in sugar output.

Countries in Africa, unlike India, did not present at the time a situation of 'surplus labour' in the Lewisian sense. Rather, they were labour shortage economies with large amount of land available for agriculture. In this situation, labour shortages caused by the pandemic deaths seem to have contributed to both contraction and compositional shift in agricultural production. Most countries experienced famine or near-famine conditions during 1918–20 because of diminished harvests (Phillips, 2017). In Lower Nigeria, peasants switched land from yam, which was traditionally considered a superior staple food, to cassava. This was because cassava required less labour to cultivate and could be grown and harvested year-round (Ohadike, 1981). In South Africa, production of maze, the main agricultural crop (that accounted for over 70 per cent of field crops) contracted by 9 per cent in 1918 and the contraction persisted until 1922 (De Kadt et al., 2021).

6.3 Non-Pharmaceutical Intervention and Economic Performance

Did restrictions imposed on social interactions through NPI measures in an attempt to slow the spread of disease impact long-term economic growth? Correia et al. (2020) examine possible mitigating effects of NPIs on the relationship between pandemic mortality rate and economic performance across US cities. The results suggest that more exposed areas experienced a sharp and persistent decline in economic activity. In particular, the pandemic reduced manufacturing output on average by 18 per cent. Cities that implemented early and extensive NPIs suffered no additional adverse economic effects from implementing those measures when compared with cities that implemented measures later or not at all. Overall, NPIs not only lower mortality but also mitigate the adverse long-term economic consequences of a pandemic. Cities that intervened earlier and more aggressively grew faster after the pandemic was over.

Ager et al. (2020): examine effects of school closures on children's educational attainment, wage income, non-wage income, and hours worked by linking data on children affected by school closure during 1918–19 in 168 cities to their adult outcomes enumerated in the 1940 census. The study failed to find any statistically significant effect of school closure on adulthood socio-economic status over and above the effect of the pandemic per se. The findings are remarkably robust to the heterogeneity of the population cohorts in terms of socio-economic status, demographic characteristics, and nativity.

Berkus et al. (2020) specifically focus on the long-term impact of NPIs' growth operating through innovation. The findings of their panel data analysis of issued patents and NPIs adopted in 50 large US cities during the pandemic suggest that cities adopting longer NPIs did not experience a decline in patenting during the pandemic relative to short-NPI cities, but recorded higher patenting afterwards. The upshot is that NPIs adopted during the pandemic may have helped preserve long-term inventive potential, rather than reduce invention by restricting localised knowledge spillover. Limiting social interactions through NPIs, presumably had positive effects on inventive activities by saving lives and reducing uncertainty, and preserving intangible organisational capital.

Noy et al. (2020) investigate the importance of the pandemic (measured by excess mortality) and NPIs in determining the economic impact of the pandemic, focussing on the production and employment in the textile industry across Japanese prefectures during 1918–20. The results suggest that there was no trade-off between economic performance and saving lives: NPIs were effective in ameliorating adverse impact of the pandemic on employment and output. Prefectures that implemented NPIs in a timely and effective manner managed to reduce the adverse impact of the pandemic on the textile industry effectively. The authors acknowledge possible endogeneity basis involved in their estimates since the imposition of NPIs arguably depends on the local mortality and morbidity rates of the pandemic. However, they argue that the endogeneity basis is unlikely to significantly distort their results given 'the relatively light touch in which the government intervened in the textile sector, and the relative low importance of the textile sector mortality in the overall mortality impact of the pandemic' (21): even though the textile industry was an important part of Japanese manufacturing, Japan was very much an agrarian economy at the time.

6.4 Pandemic and Socio-economic Status

A view central to the hysterography of pandemics and natural disasters is the importance of socio-economic status in understanding their unequal impact on the populace (Ferguson, 2021; Scheidel, 2017). The available, albeit limited, evidence relating to the 1918–20 pandemic is consistent with this view: throughout the world, a higher incidence of pandemic mortality was experienced by those classes and communities that normally had the weakest grip on life (Johnson, 2006; Kraut, 2010; Mamelund, 2006, 2018; Mills, 1986; Pool, 1973; Sydenstricker, 1931).

In England there was somewhat higher mortality in the poorest, least salubrious parts of London, even though correlation with wealth was not specifically strong (Johnson, 2006). A survey conducted by the US Public Health Service in nine urban localities in the United States showed that there were marked and consistent differences in the incidence of morbidity and mortality among persons of differing economic statuses. The lower the economic level, the higher the attack rate. This pattern was found to persist even after allowances had been made for factors of colour, sex, age, and certain other conditions (Sydenstricker, 1931). A study of social status and pandemic deaths in Norway found that household wealth and social status of place of residence had a significant and independent effect on mortality after controlling for age, sex, and marital status. The poor came down with influenza first, while the rich with less exposure in the first wave had the highest morbidity in the second wave. The impact of the pandemic was most severe among transport, hotel, and industry workers (Mamelund, 2018).

Fourie and Jayes (2020) found that in South Africa pre-existing racial disparities in access to healthcare were responsible for disparities in influenza mortality across communities and that the pandemic only served to widen prior racial disparities in health. In the United States, newly arrived migrants suffered more (Kraut, 2010), and death rates were much higher among native Indians (Crosby, 2003). In Paris, domestic servants figured prominently among the dead compared to affluent citizens (McBride, 1976). In New Zealand, the death toll was much higher among the Maori population compared to the non-Maori majority population[28] (Pool, 1973; Rice, 1988: Chapter 6). The Inuit and

---

[28] The official Maori death rate (2.26 per cent) was five times the European rate (Rice 1988: 102).

other indigenous people suffered much higher mortality in Canada (Johnson, 2006). Indentured labourers in the plantation sector of Ceylon (Sri Lanka), who were drawn from the lowest echelons of South Indian society and lived in poor and cramped conditions in plantations, suffered more than the other communities in the country (Langford & Storey, 1992; Killingray, 2003).

If socio-economic status is a key determinant of the severity of the impact of the pandemic, one would have expected the Black population in the United States to be the worst affected compared to the White. In a review of the literature on the relationship between race and mortality during the 1918–20 pandemic, Crosby (2003) noted that the Black population, in fact, had lower morbidity and mortality compared to the White population. Crosby's explanation for this was that Black people were more exposed to a mild spring/summer wave of influenza earlier that same year. In a recent study of Black–White difference in the pandemic impact, Økland and Mamelund (2019) find that the Black population had both lower morbidity and mortality as observed by Crosby, but higher case fatality than the White population. The results seem to suggest that Black people had a lower risk of developing the disease given their early exposure to the first wave, but when they did get sick, they had a higher risk of dying. De Kadt et al., (2021) find that in South Africa poor access to medical services was an important reason for the higher incidence of pandemic death among Black people compared to the White population. According to their analysis of death certificates of pandemic deaths, there was evidence of doctor presence in only 10 per cent of Black deaths compared to 39 per cent of White deaths.

Galletta et al. (2020) estimate the effect of the 1918 Influenza pandemic on income inequality in Italian municipalities using newly digitised historical administrative records of Italian taxpayer incomes. The findings suggest that in the short to medium term (within five years) income inequality is higher in municipalities with higher pandemic death rates, and the effect is mostly explained by a reduction in the share of income held by poorer people.

In India 'almost from the outset influenza was described as really a disease of hunger and exhaustion' (Arnold, 2019: 192). The people who suffered most were the poor and rural classes whose housing conditions, medical attendance, food, and clothing were in deficit. The administrative reports of the colonial administration almost universally emphasised a strong correlation between poverty, deprivation, and debility on the one hand and influenza fatality on the other (Phipson, 1923). In Bombay (modern-day Mumbai) the mortality rate of lower-caste Hindus was three times higher than that of other Hindus and eight times higher than Europeans (Mills, 1986). In Malawi (Nyasaland) there was a large difference in mortality rate between the Europe and local people (Sambala, 2012). A similar difference was observed in Korea between Japanese citizens and the native Koreans (Lim, 2011).

7 Lessons

The Great Influenza Pandemic of 1918–20 is by far the most devastating of all pandemics in modern history. Even at a time when shipping was the sole mode of international travel, the 1918–20 pandemic was able to affect the whole civilised world. A high fatality rate, which was over 20 times higher than expected in a normal influenza season, the high incidence of death among people of prime age, and a short and abrupt ending were its hallmarks that have not yet been fully understood by epidemiologists. The last year of WW1 coincided with the first year of the pandemic and facilitated the initial spread of the virus and perhaps mutation of the virus into a more virulent form, but the pandemic was not simply a war epidemic. The brunt of the cost of the pandemic was borne by the countries in the world periphery (the present-day developing countries). Even though the pandemic abruptly ended in less than one year in the Western world, it lingered on into 1920 in some parts of the developing world.

The H1N1 virus that caused the 1918–20 pandemic turned out to be a 'foundation virus', descendants of which persist to this date. All influenza pandemics since that time, and almost all cases of influenza worldwide (except human infections from avian viruses such as H5N1 and H7N7), have been caused by descendants of the 1918 virus, making the 1918 virus the 'mother of all pandemics' (Taubenberger & Morens, 2006: 70). Whether the virus of the COVID-19 pandemic, SARS-COVID 2, too, will persist as a foundation virus, or die out in the face of growing population immunity associated with natural infection and new COVID-19 vaccines is bound to be a perplexing issue for the medical researchers in years to come (Morens et al., 2021).

We live in a time when the world is far more susceptible to 'unification by infectious disease' than it was in the early twentieth century. The speed and extent of the global spread of the COVID-19 virus have therefore been unparalleled in world history. However, the current pandemic arrived at a time of remarkable medical advances: rapid viral diagnostics, diagnostic imaging, antibiotics, antivirals, intensive care units with ventilators with membrane oxygenation, and, most importantly, advances in virology that have fostered the development of a vaccine. Therefore, the indications are that, contrary to some alarming predictions, the mortality rate of the COVID-19 pandemic is unlikely to be as high as that of the 1918–20 pandemic.[29] The socio-economic cost is likely to be determined, therefore, by morbidity rather than mortality and economic disruption associated with NPIs including social distancing and shutting down economic activity.

---

[29] By the end of October 2021, world mortality rate of the COVID-19 pandemic was only 0.06 per cent, compared to an attack rate of 3.1 per cent: the case mortality rate stood at 2 per cent. (https://coronavirus.jhu.edu/map.html)

Since the vast majority of infected people would ultimately survive, the impact of morbidity on the demographic dynamic and human capital development is likely to dominate the post-pandemic research agenda. The sizeable literature spawned by the 1918–20 pandemic on this subject is bound to attract much attention in post-COVD-19 research. Research pertaining to the impact of maternal and fetal risk, and temporal and cross-disease mortality spillover on human capital development is going to be of particular relevance in this connection (Moren et al., 2021).

Regardless of the pathology of a pandemic, its impacts are often a function of socio-economic conditions. The impact of the virus itself will be compounded by the socio-economic conditions and state capacity (political order). It is as much the social networks and state capacities that the pathogen encounters that determine the magnitude of a pandemic's socio-economic impact: the virus will infect only as many people as these preconditions permit.

Perhaps the most important lesson arising out of the 1918–20 pandemic for the COVID-19 policy debate relates to unequal distribution of burden between developed and developing countries. At a time when existing therapeutic intervention made little difference, inter-country differences in the death toll of the global influenza pandemic of 1918–20 were strongly mediated by the state of economic advancement, with poverty and deprivation and associated comorbidity playing a vital role over and above the virulence of the virus. The global experience vividly illustrated that mortality caused by a pandemic is mostly a reflection of the socio-economic and political order that the pathogen encounters not its virulence per se. Whether advances in medical intervention will assist in reducing the unequal distribution of the overall impact of the pandemic and mortality outcomes remains debatable and to be seen.

Vaccines are obviously the cornerstone in our flight against viral disease. The speedy development of effective vaccines within less than a year of the onset of the pandemic is a steller achievement of modern viral research spawned by the 1918–20 pandemic. A pivotal policy issue is how new medicines and vaccines against COVID-19 are going to be distributed. Issues of patenting and the monopolistic practices of pharmaceutical markets that are dominated by multi-national enterprises are directly relevant here (Stiglitz et al., 2020). For instance, relating to the HIV/AIDS pandemic, quickly identifying the virus and developing antiretroviral therapy was widely cited as an example of the power of modern medical research (what can happen in an outbreak of infectious disease) (Deaton, 2013). However, it took many years for the benefits to trickle down to the developing world. An estimated 37.9 million people are still living with HIV/AIDS (Fauci & Lane, 2020), and 570,000 to 1.1 million people are still dying from the disease annually, most of them in developing countries, with

African countries alone accounting for 61 per cent of deaths.[30] Under the normal market mechanisms, vaccines and large stocks of antibiotics or antivirals are unlikely to be available in most low-income countries.

The remarkable propensity of viruses to mutate and their unpredictable dissipation as seen in the course of the 1918–20 pandemic has implications for public policy relating to vaccine development, production, and equitable worldwide distribution. A vast body of knowledge on the structure and habits of the flu virus has evolved over the past hundred years, but the virus can frustrate our best efforts by changing its salient features faster than we can recognise the changes, essentially meaning that 'the virus will be one step ahead of the vaccine manufacturers' (Burnet & White, 1972: 212). Moreover, the possibility of abrupt dissipation and uncertainty of duration of the pandemic makes massive investment in vaccine development risky from a private enterprise perspective.[31] The upshot is that governments and international developmental organisations have to play an important role to alleviate the commercial risk involved in the development and production of vaccines that the pharmaceutical companies are naturally hesitant to bear on their own.

In a context where the whole world is in the midst of a pandemic, responsible national and international developmental organisations have to take risks on behalf of the public. It is better to err on the side of overreaction than under-reaction. Even if the wealthy countries emerge victorious from the COVID-19 war, the victory would be short-lived in this era of economic and social globalisation if the pandemic continues to cause havoc elsewhere.

As Osterholm and Olshaker (2020) have aptly put it, COVID-19 is in fact 'the pandemic foretold'. As we have discussed at the outset of this Element, there were ample pre-warnings about the coming disaster two or so decades before the onset of the pandemic. These warnings did not lead to pandemic preparedness actions, presumably because the individual governments and international organisations remained preoccupied with one global risk, namely climate change. The COVID-19 disaster reinforces the case of bringing pandemic risk and pandemic preparedness to the forefront of international development agenda given that the whole world is now a 'single epidemiological unit'. The 1918–20 pandemic was the harbinger of the rise of virology as a dominant sub-area within epidemiology. The COVID-19 pandemic is bound to elevate 'economics of infectious disease' to the forefront of scientific research and public policy debate.

---

[30] www.who.int/gho/hiv/epidemic_status/deaths_text/en

[31] Following the outbreak of swine flu in 1976, pharmaceutical companies spent millions of dollars in production and distribution of a new flu vaccine, but the flu did not trigger a pandemic as predicted (Crosby, 2003: xii; Sencer and Millar, 2006).

Appendix

Mortality of the 1918–20 influenza pandemic

	Death (thousands)[a]	Mortality rate (%)
Africa	2,565–2,658	3.1–3.2
Belgian Congo	300	5.0
Botswana	7	4.0
Cameroon	25	4.5
Egypt	139–170	1.1–1.3
Gambia	8	3.7
Gold Coast (Ghana)	89–100	3.9–4.4
Kenya	150	5.8
Madagascar	119	3.5
Mauritius	12	3.2
Nigeria	455	2.4
Nyasaland (Malavi)	120	9.8
Senegal	38	3.0
Sierra Leone	46	3.0
South Africa	300	4.4
Southern Rhodesia	38	4.4
Tanganyika (Tanzania)	100	2.1
Other	620	3.3–3.5
Middle East	910	8.1
Iran	910	8.1
Latin America	800–1,053	1.1–1.5
Argentina	10.2–46	0.1–0.5
British Caribbean	30	1.5
Caribbean other	70	1.4
Brazil	180.0	0.7
Chile	20–35	0.5–0.9
Guatemala	49	3.9
Columbia	27	0.5
Mexico	300–500	2.1–3.4
Peru[b]	4	1.6
Uruguay	2.1–2.4	0.1–0.3

(cont.)

	Death (thousands)[a]	Mortality rate (%)
Venezuela	12	0.4
Asia	24,232–32,498	2.5–3.5
East Asia	4,664–10,305	0.9–1.9
Japan	453–517	0.8–0.9
China	4,000–9,500	0.8–2.0
Korea	185–235	1.1–1.4
Taiwan	26–53	0.7–1.4
Southeast Asia	1,719–2,049	2.4–2.9
Indonesia	1500–1630	3.0–3.3
Malaysia	40–43	1.2–1.3
Philippines	94–288	0.9–2.8
Singapore	5–7	1.3–1.8
Thailand	80–82	0.9–1.0
South Asia	17,097–18,890	5.4–6.0
Afghanistan	320	5.5
British India[c]	16,700–18,500	5.5–6.1
Ceylon (Sri Lanka)	77–80	1.7–1.8
North America	588–901	0.5–0.8
Canada	51	0.6
USA	537–850	0.5–0.8
Europe	5,069–5865	1.0–1.1
Austria	21–98	0.3–1.6
Belgium	64	0.8
Czechia[d]	72	0.7
Croatia	109	3.6
Denmark	6	0.2
Eire (Ireland)	18	0.4
England and Wales	156–200	0.5–0.6
Finland	18–26	0.6–0.8
France	240	0.7
Germany	225–444	0.4–0.8
Greece	25	0.5
Prussia	237	0.5
Hungary	100	1.3
Island	1	0.6
Italy	390–501	1.1–1.4
Netherlands	48	0.7
Norway	15	0.6
Portugal	59–158	1.0–2.6

(cont.)

	Death (thousands)[a]	Mortality rate (%)
Russia (USSR)[e]	2,760	1.5[d]
Scotland	28–34	0.6–0.7
Spain	257–311	1.2–1.5
Sweden	34–28	0.6–0.7
Switzerland	23–26	0.6–0.7
Turkey	162–221	1.1–1.5
Oceania	42–45	0.6–0.7
Australia	15	0.3
New Zealand	44	0.6–0.7
Fiji	9	5.5
Tonga	1	3.9–7.8
Western Samoa	9	23.6
Country total	35,158–44,881	2.0–2.6
World total[f]	37,095–47,353	2.0–2.6
Memorandum items[g]		
Developing countries	30,065–38,990	2.5–3.2
Developed countries	5,092–5890	1.0–1.1

Note: [a] regional totals include estimates by Johnson and Muller (2002) for other countries in the region (after deducting deaths of countries newly added). [b] Covers three main cities (Lima, Liquito, and Ica) only. [c] Includes Burma (Myanmar), Pakistan and Bangladesh. [d] Parts of Austria-Hungary, the Czech parts of former Czechoslovakia, and the modern state of Czechia. [e] Based on Russian-language sources summarised in Slomczynski (2012). [f] Country total extrapolated by the population share of the countries covered (94 per cent). [g] Countries classified based on the UN Standard Country Classification. www.un.org/en/development/desa/policy/wesp/; wesp_current/2014wesp_country_classification.pdf

Source: Johnson and Muller (2002) (based on a survey of literature on the subject published during 1920 to 1998); Afkhami (2003): Iran; Andayi et al. (2019): Kenya; Ansart et al. (2009): Europe; Alexander (2019): Mexico; Barro et al. (2020): 43 countries; Beach et al. (2020): USA; Chowell et al. (2011): Peru; Chowell et al. (2014): Chile; Feldman (2014): Argentina; Gealogo (2009): Philippines; Gaddy (2021): Czechia; Hayami (2015): Japan; Karsson et al. (2014): Sweden; Killingray (1994): Caribbean Islands; Killingray (2003): Tanganyika; Kim (2011): Korea; Lee et al. (2007): Singapore; Liew (2007): Malaysia; Murray et al. (2006): 27 countries; National Museum of Australia (undated) and Curson and McCracken (2006): Australia; Royal Thai Government (1919): Thailand; Rose (2021): Egypt; Sambala (2012): Nyasaland.

References

Afkhami, A. (2003). Compromised constitutions: The Iranian experience with the 1918 influenza pandemic. *Bulletin of the History of Medicine*, 77(2), 367–92. https://doi.org/10.1353/bhm.2003.0049

Ager, P., Eriksson, K., Karger, E., Nencka, P., & Thomasson, M. A. (2020). School closures during the 1918 flu pandemic. *Working Paper No. 28246*. Cambridge, MA: National Bureau of Economic Research.

Alexander, R. M. (2019). The Spanish Flu and the sanitary dictatorship: Mexico's response to the 1918 influenza pandemic. *The Americas*, 76(3), 443–65. https://doi.org/10.1017/tam.2019.34

Alfani, G. & Murphy, T. E. (2017). Plague and lethal epidemics in the pre-industrial world. *Journal of Economic History*, 77(1), 314–43. https://doi .org/10.1017/S0022050717000092

Almond, D. (2006). Is the 1918 influenza pandemic over? Long-term effects of in utero influenza exposure in the post-1940 US population. *Journal of Political Economy*, 114(4), 672–712. https://doi.org/10.1086/507154

Almond, D. & Currie, J. (2011). Killing me softly: The fetal origins hypothesis. *Journal of Economic Perspectives*, 25(3), 153–72. https://doi.org/10.1257/ jep.25.3.153

Almond, D. & Mazumder, B. (2005). The 1918 influenza pandemic and subsequent health outcomes: An analysis of SIPP data. *American Economic Review*, 95(2), 258–62. https://doi.org/10.1257/000282805774669943

Andayi, F., Chaves, S. S. & Widdowson, M.-A. (2019). Impact of the 1918 influenza pandemic in coastal Kenya. *Tropical Medicine and Infectious Disease*, 4(2), 9–12. https://doi.org/10.3390/tropicalmed4020091

Ansart, S., Pelat, C., Boelle, P.-Y. et al. (2009). Mortality burden of the 1918–1919 influenza pandemic in Europe. *Influenza and Other Respiratory Viruses*, 3(3), 99–106. https://doi.org/10.1111/j.1750-2659.2009.00080.x

Arnold, D. (1988). Introduction: Disease, medicine and Empire. In D. Arnold, ed., *Imperial Medicine and Indigenous Societies*, Manchester: Manchester University Press, pp. 1–26.

Arnold, D. (2019). Death and the modern empire: The 1918-19 influenza pandemic in India. *Transactions of the Royal Historical Society*, 29(1), 181–200. https://doi.org/10.1017/S0080440119000082

Arnold, D. (2020). Pandemic India: Coronavirus and the uses of history. *The Journal of Asian Studies* 79(3), 569–77.

Aron, J. & Muelbauer, J. (2020). A pandemic primer on excess mortality statistics and their comparability across countries. *Our World Today.* https://ourworldindata.org/covid-excess-mortality (accessed 9 September 2020).

Arthi, V. & Parman, J. (2021). Disease, downturns, and wellbeing: Economic history and the long-run impacts of COVID-19. *Explorations in Economic History*, 79(1), 9–23. https://doi.org/10.1016/j.eeh.2020.101381

Asquith, B. J. (2020). What can we learn from the 1918 pandemic? Careful economics and policy lessons from influenza. *Policy Paper No. 2020-022.* Kalamazoo, MI: W.E. Upjohn Institute for Employment Research. http://doi.org/10.17848/pol2020-022

Balfour, A. & Scott, H. H. (1924). *Health Problems of the Empire: Past, Present, and Future.* London: W. Collins and Son.

Barker, D. J. (1992). The fetal origins of diseases of old age. *European Journal of Clinical Nutrition*, 46(3), S3–S9.

Barro, R. J. (2020). Non-pharmaceutical interventions and mortality in US cities during the great influenza pandemic, 1918-1919. *Working Paper 27049.* Cambridge, MA: National Bureau of Economic Research (NBER). https://doi.org/10.3386/w27049

Barro, R. J., Ursúa, J. F., & Weng, J. (2020). The coronavirus and the great influenza pandemic: Lessons from the 'Spanish Flu' for the coronavirus's potential effects on mortality and economic activity. *Working Paper 26866.* Cambridge, MA: National Bureau of Economic Research (NBER). https://doi.org/10.3386/w26866

Barry, J. M. (2004a). *The Great Influenza: The Epic Story of the Deadliest Plague in History.* New York: Viking Penguin.

Barry, J. M. (2004b). The site of origin of the 1918 influenza pandemic and its public health implications. *Journal of Transnational Medicine*, 2(1), 1–4.

Basco, S., Domènech, J., & Rosés, J. R. (2021). The redistributive effects of pandemics: Evidence on the Spanish flu. *World Development*, 141, 105389.

Beach, B., Clay, K., & Saavedra, M. H. (2020). The 1918 influenza pandemic and its lessons for COVID-19. *Journal of Economic Literature*, 60 (1), 41–84.

Beach, B., Ferrie, J. P., & Saavedra, M. H. (2018). Fetal shock or selection? The 1918 influenza pandemic and human capital development. *Working Paper 24725.* Cambridge, MA: National Bureau of Economic Research (NBER). https://doi.org/10.3386/w24725

Belling, C. (2009). Overwhelming the medium: Fiction and the trauma of pandemic influenza in 1918. *Literature and Medicine*, 28(1), 55–81.

Berkes, E., Deschenes. O., Gaetani, R., Lin, J., & Severen, C. (2020). Lockdowns and innovation: Evidence from the 1918 flu pandemic. *Working Paper No. 28152*. Cambridge, MA: National Bureau of Economic Research (NBER).

British Medical Journal (BMJ) (1919). Influenza in Samoa: Value of vaccines. *BMJ* 2(3068), 499–500.

Boberg-Fazlic, N., Ivets, M., Karlsson, M., & Nilsson, T. (2021). Disease and fertility: Evidence from the 1918–19 influenza pandemic in Sweden. *Economics & Human Biology,* 43, 101020.

Bolanovsky, M. & Erreygers, G. (2021). How economists ignored the Spanish Flu pandemic in 1918–1920. *Erasmus Journal for Philosophy and Economics,* 14(1), 89–109.

Bootsma, M. C. J. & Ferguson, N. M. (2007). The effect of public health measures on the 1918 influenza pandemic in US cities. *Proceedings of the National Academy of Sciences,* 104(8), 7588–93. https://doi.org/10.1073/pnas.0611071104

Brainerd, E., & Siegler M. V. (2003). The economic effects of the 1918 influenza epidemic. *Working Paper 3791.* London: Centre for Economic Policy Research. SSRN: https://papers.ssrn.com/soL3/papers.cfm?abstract_id=394606.

Brown, C. (1987). The influenza pandemic of 1918 in Indonesia. In N. Oeven, ed., *Death and Disease in Southeast Asia: Explorations in Social, Medical and Demographic History.* Singapore: Oxford University, pp. 235–56.

Burnet, F. M. (1953). *Natural History of Infectious Disease,* 2nd ed. Cambridge: Cambridge University Press.

Burnet, F. M. (1979). Portraits of viruses: Influenza virus A. *Intervirology,* 11(4), 201–14. https://doi.org/10.1159/000149035

Burnet, F. M. & Clark, E. (1942). *Influenza: A Survey of the Last 50 Years in the Light of Modern Work on the Virus of Epidemic Influenza.* Melbourne: Macmillan.

Burnet, F. M. & White, D. O. (1972). *Natural History of Infectious Disease,* 4th ed. Cambridge: Cambridge University Press.

Burns, A. F. & Mitchell, W. C. (1946). *Measuring Business Cycles.* New York: National Bureau of Economic Research.

Byerly, C. R. (2005). *Fever of War: The Influenza Epidemic in the U.S. Army during the World War 1.* New York: New York University Press.

Carillo, M. F. & Jappelli, T. (2020). Pandemics and local economic growth: Evidence from the great influenza in Italy. *Paper No. DP14849.* London: Centre for Economic Policy Research.

Chandra, S. (2013). Mortality from the influenza pandemic of 1918–19 in Indonesia. *Population Studies,* 67(2), 185–93

Chandra, S. & Christensen, J. (2017). Preparing for pandemic influenza: The Global 1918 Influenza pandemic and the role of world historical information. *Journal of World-Historical Information*, 3–4(1), 20–30. https://doi.org/10.5195/jwhi.2017.45

Chandra, S., Christensen, J., Mamelund, S.-E. & Paneth, N. (2018). Short-term birth sequelae of the 1918-1920 influenza pandemic in the United States: State-level analysis. *American Journal of Epidemiology*, 187(12), 2585–95.

Chandra, S. & Kassens-Noor, E. (2014). The evolution of pandemic influenza: Evidence from India, 1918–19'. *BMC Infectious Diseases*, 14(1), 510–20. https://doi.org/10.1186/1471-2334-14-510

Chandra, S., Kuljanin, G., & Wray, J. (2012). Mortality from the influenza pandemic of 1918–1919: The case of India. *Demography*, 49(3), 857–65. https://doi.org/10.1007/s13524-012-0116-x

Chandra, S. & Sarathchandra, D. (2014). The influenza pandemic of 1918–1919 in Sri Lanka: Its demographic cost, timing, and propagation. *Influenza and Other Respiratory Viruses*, 8(3), 267–73. https://doi.org/10.1111/irv.12238

Chandra, S. & Yu, Y.-L. (2015a). Fertility decline and the 1918 influenza pandemic in Taiwan. *Biodemography and Social Biology*, 61(3), 266–72. https://doi.org/10.1080/19485565.2015.1062718

Chandra, S. & Yu, Y.-L. (2015b). The 1918 influenza pandemic and subsequent birth deficit in Japan. *Demographic Research*, 33, 313–26. https://doi.org/10.4054/DemRes.2015.33.11

Cheng, K. F. & Leung, P. C. (2007). What happened in China during the 1918 influenza pandemic?' *International Journal of Infectious Diseases*, 11(4), 360–4. https://doi.org/10.1016/j.ijid.2006.07.009

Chowell, G., Simonsen, L., Flores, J., Miller, M. A. & Viboud, C. (2014). Death patterns during the 1918 influenza pandemic in Chile. *Emerging Infectious Diseases*, 20(11), 1803–11. https://doi.org/10.3201/eid2011.130632

Chowell, G., Viboud, C., Simonsen, L. et al. (2011). The 1918–1920 influenza pandemic in Peru'. *Vaccine*, 29(2011), B21–B26. https://doi.org/10.1016/j.vaccine.2011.02.048

Christopher, A. J. (1992). Ethnicity, community and the census in Mauritius, 1930-1990. *The Royal Geographical Society*, 18(1), 57–64.

Collier, R. (1974). *The Plague of the Spanish Lady: The Influenza Pandemic of 1918–29*. London: Macmillan.

Collins, S. D. (1931). Age and sex incidence of influenza and pneumonia morbidity and mortality in the epidemic of 1928-29 with comparative data for the epidemic of 1918. *Public Health Reports*, 46(33), 1909–37.

Cook, C., Justin, F., Fletcher, J., & Forgues, A. (2019). Multigenerational effects of early-life health shocks. *Demography*, 56, 1855–74.

Correia, S., Luck, S., & Verner, E. (2020). Pandemics depresses the economy, public health interventions do not: Evidence from the 1918 Flu. *SSRN Electronic Journal.* https://doi.org/10.2139/ssrn.3561560

Crosby, A. W. (2003). *America's Forgotten Pandemic: The Influenza of 1918*, 2nd ed. Cambridge: Cambridge University Press. https://doi.org/10.1017/CBO9780511586576

Curson, P. & McCracken, K. (2006). An Australian perspective of the 1918–1919 influenza pandemic. *New South Wales Public Health Bulletin*, 17(8), 103–7. https://doi.org/10.1071/NB06025

da Costa, V. G., Moreli, M. L., & Saivish, M. V. (2020). The emergence of SARS, MERS and Novel SARS-2 coronaviruses in the 21st century. *Archives of Virology*, 165(7), 1517–26. https://doi.org/10.1007/s00705-020-04628-0

Dahl, C. M., Hansen, W. & Jense, P. S. (2020). The 1918 epidemic and a V-shaped recession: Evidence from municipal income data. *Covid Economics*, 6(2020), 137–62.

Davis, K. (1951). *The Population of India and Pakistan.* Princeton: Princeton University Press.

Deaton, A. (2013). *The Great Escape: Health, Wealth, and the Origins of Inequality.* Princeton: Princeton University Press. https://doi.org/10.1515/9781400847969

de Kadt, D., Fourie, J., Greyling, J., Murard, E., & Norling, J. (2021). Correlates and Consequences of the 1918 Influenza in South Africa. *African Journal of Economics*, 89(2),173–95.

Donaldson, D. & Keniston, D. (2016). Dynamics of a Malthusian economy: India in the aftermath of the 1918 influenza. *Unpublished Manuscript.* www.lsu.edu/business/economics/files/microecon-conf-lsu-keniston.pdf

Ewald, P. W. (1994). *Evolution of Infectious Diseases.* Oxford: Oxford University Press.

Ewald, P. W. (2011). Evolution of virulence, environmental change, and the threat posed by emerging and chronic diseases. *Ecological Research*, 26, 1017–26. https://doi.org/10.1007/s11284-011-0874-8

Fan, V. Y., Jamison, D. T., & Summers, L. H. (2018) Pandemic risk: How large are the expected lossless? *Bulletin of the World Health Organization*, 96, 129–34.

Fauci, A. S. & Lane, H. C. (2020). Four decades of HIV/AIDS: Much accomplished, much to do. *New England Journal of Medicine*, 383(1), 1–4. https://doi.org/10.1056/NEJMp1916753

Feldman, H. (2014). The Spanish Flu in Argentina: Alarming hostage. In M. I. Porras-Gallo & R. A. Davis, eds., *The Spanish Influenza Pandemic of*

1918-1919: Perspectives from the Iberian Peninsula and the Americas. Rochester: University of Rochester Press, pp.194–215.

Fenske, J., Gupta, B., & Yuan, S. (2020). Demographic shocks and women's labor market participation: Evidence from the 1918 influenza pandemic in India. *Discussion Paper No. DP15077*. London: Center for Economic Policy Research. https://papers.ssrn.com/sol3/papers.cfm?abstract_id=3661420.

Ferguson, N. (2021), *Doom: The Politics of Catastrophe.* New York: Allen Lane.

Ferguson, N., Laydon, D. I., Gilani, G. N. et al. (2020). Report 9: Impact of non-pharmaceutical interventions (NPIs) to reduce COVID19 mortality and health-care Demand. *Imperial College London.* https://pdfs.semanticscholar.org/8c73/19446bd3e435ede14852e22be6b60b6f5127.pdf

Fletcher, J. (2018). The effects of *in utero* exposure to the 1918 influenza pandemic on family formation. *Economics and Human Biology*, 30(1), 59–68.

Fourie, J. & Jayes, J. (2020). Health inequality and the 1918 influenza in South Africa. Mimeo (as cited in Arthi and Parman 2021).

Frost, W. H. (1920). Statistics of influenza morbidity: With special reference to certain factors in case incidence and case fatality. *Public Health Reports*, 35(11), 584–97. https://doi.org/10.2307/4575511

Gaddy, H. G. (2021). Excess mortality during the 1918-20 influenza pandemic in Czechia. *medRxiv* (The Printing Server for Health Science) www.medrxiv.org/content/10.1101/2021.01.10.21249537v1.full.pdf (2021).

Gagnon, A., Miller, M. S., Hallman, S. A. et al. (2013). Age-specific mortality during the 1918 influenza pandemic: Unravelling the mystery of high young adult mortality. *PLOS ONE*, 8(8), 1–10. https://doi.org/10.1371/journal.pone.0069586.

Gallardo-Albarrán, D. & de Zwart, P. (2021). A bitter epidemic: The impact of the 1918 influenza on sugar production in Java. *Economics & Human Biology*, 42(1), 1–18.

Galletta, S. & Giommoni, T. (2020). 'The effect of the 1918 influenza pandemic on income inequality: Evidence from Italy. *SSRN 3634793*.

Gardiner, P. & Oey, M. (1987). Morbidity and mortality in Java 1980-1940: The evidence of the colonial reports. In N. Oven, ed., *Death and Disease in Southeast Asia: Explorations in Social, Medical and Demographic History.* Singapore: Oxford University, pp. 70–90.

Garrett, L. (2005). The next pandemic? *Foreign Affairs*, July/August, 84, 3–23. https://doi.org/10.2307/20034417

Garrett, T. A. (2007). *Economic effects of the 1918 Influenza Pandemic: Implications for a Modern-Day Pandemic.* St. Louis, Missouri: Federal Reserve Bank of St. Louis. www.stlouisfed.org/community/other_pubs.html

Garrett, T. A. (2009). War and pestilence as labor market shocks: US manufacturing wage growth 1914–1919. *Economic Inquiry*, 47(4), 711–25. https://doi .org/10.1111/j.1465-7295.2008.00137.x

Gassem, L. B. (2020). Spanish flu: How the deadly pandemic affected the Arab World. *Arab News*. www.arabnews.com/node/1649051/saudi-arabia (accessed 8 September 2020).

Gealogo, F. A. (2009). The Philippines in the world of the influenza pandemic of 1918-1919. *Philippines Studies*, 57(2), 261–92.

Gewald, J.-B. (2007). Spanish influenza in Africa: Some Comments Regarding Source material and Future research. *ASC Working Paper 77/2007*. Leiden: African Studies Centre.

Gill, C. A. (1928). *The Genesis of Epidemics and the Natural History of Disease. An Introduction to the Science of Epidemiology Based Upon the Study of Epidemics of Malaria, Influenza, and Plague*. Kent: Baillière Tindall & Cox.

Gladwell, M. (1997). The deadliest virus ever know zone. *The New Yorker*, 22 September. www.newyorker.com/magazine/1997/09/29/the-dead-zone (accessed September 2020).

Government of India. (1924). *The Census of India 1921* (Part 1). Calcutta: Superintendent of Government.

Government of India. (1938). *Annual Report of the Public Health Commissioner with the Government of India for 1936*. New Delhi: Government of India Central Publication Branch.

Gregoer, M. (2020). *How to Survive a Pandemic*. London: Pan Macmillan/ Bluebird.

Guimbeau, A., Menon, N., & Musacchio, A. (2020). The Brazilian bombshell? the long-term impact of the 1918 influenza pandemic the south American way. *Working Paper No.26929*. Cambridge, MA: National Bureau of Economic Research.

Gulland, A. (2016). World invests too little and is underprepared for disease outbreaks, report Warns. *British Medical Journal*, 352, 225). https://doi.org/ 10.1136/bmj.i225.

Hampton, J. R. (1998). The end of medical history? *Journal of the Royal College of Physicians of London*, 32(4), 366–75.

Hatchett, R. J., Mecher, C. E., & Lipsitch, M. (2007). Public health interventions and epidemic intensity during the 1918 influenza pandemic. *Proceedings of the National Academy of Sciences*, 104(18), 7582–7.

Hayami, A. (2015). *The Influenza in Japan, 1918–1920: The first world war between humankind and virus*. Translated by L. E. Riggs & M. Takechi. Tokyo: International Research Centre for Japanese Studies.

Helgertz, J. & Bengtsson, T. (2019). The Long-lasting influenza: The impact of fetal stress during the 1918 influenza pandemic on socioeconomic attainment and health in Sweden, 1968–2012. *Demography*, 56(4), 1389–425. https://doi .org/10.1007/s13524-019-00799-x

Hill, K. (2011). Influenza in India 1918: excess mortality reassessed. *Genus*, 67(2), 9–29.

Hollenbeck, J. E. (2005). An avian connection as a catalyst to the 1918-1919 influenza pandemic. *International Journal of Medical Sciences*, 2(2), 87–92.

Honigsbaum, M. (2020). *A History of the Great Influenza Pandemic: Death, Panic and Hysteria, 1983–1920*. London: Bloomsbury.

Humphries, M. (2014). Paths of infection: The first World War and the origins of the 1918 influenza pandemic. *War in History*, 21(1), 55–81 https://doi.org/10 .1177%2F0968344513504525

Iijima, W. (2003). Snappish influenza in China, 1918-1920: A preliminary probe. In D. Killingray & H. Phillip, eds., *The Spanish Flu Pandemic of 1918: New Perspectives*. London: Routledge, pp. 101–9.

Jefferson, T. & Ferroni, E. (2009). The Spanish influenza pandemic seen through the *BMJ*'s eyes: Observations and unanswered questions. *British Medical Journal*, 339, 5313–6. https://doi.org/10.1136/bmj.b5313

Jester, B., Uyeki, T., &Jernigan, D. (2018). Readiness for responding to a severe pandemic 100 years after 1918. *American Journal of Epidemiology*, 187(12), 2596–602.

Johnson, N. (2006). *Britain and the 1918–19 Influenza Pandemic: A Dark Epilogue*. London: Routledge. https://doi.org/10.4324/9780203018163

Johnson, N. & Mueller, J. (2002). Updating the accounts: Global mortality of the 1918-1920 'Spanish' influenza pandemic. *Bulletin of the History of Medicine*, 76(1), 105–15. https://doi.org/10.1353/bhm.2002.0022

Jones, D. S. (2020). History in a crisis: Lessons for Covid-19. *New England Journal of Medicine*, 382(18), 1681–3. https://doi.org/10.1056/NEJMp2004361

Jordà, Ò, Singh, S. R., & Taylor, A. M. (2022). Longer-run economic consequences of pandemics? *The Review of Economics and Statistics* (preview), 104(1), 166–75. https://doi.org/10.1162/rest_a_01042

Jordan, D. (2020). The deadliest flu: The complete story of the discovery and reconstruction of the 1918 pandemic virus. Washington, DC: Centres for Disease Control and Prevention. www.cdc.gov/flu/pandemic-resources/ reconstruction-1918-virus.html

Jordan, E. O. (1927). *Epidemic Influenza: A Survey*. Chicago: American Medical Association.

Karlsson, M., Nilsson, T. & Pichler, S. (2014). The impact of the 1918 Spanish flu epidemic on economic performance in Sweden: An investigation into the consequences of an extraordinary mortality shock. *Journal of Health Economics*, 36, 1–19.

Kermack, W. O. & McKendrick, A. G. (1927). A contribution to the mathematical theory of epidemics. *Proceedings of the royal society of London. Series A, Containing Papers of a Mathematical and Physical Character*, 115(772), 700–21.

Kilbourne, E. D. (2006). Influenza pandemics of the 20th century. *Emerging Infectious Diseases*, 12(1), 10–14.

Killingray, D. (1994). The influenza pandemic of 1918–1919 in the British Caribbean. *Social History and Medicine*, 7, 59–87. https://doi.org/10.1093/shm/7.1.59

Killingray, D. (2003). A new imperial disease: The influenza pandemic of 1918–9 and its impact on the British Empire. *Caribbean Quarterly*, 49(4), 30–49. https://doi.org/10.1080/00086495.2003.11829645

Klein, I. (1973). Death in India, 1871–1921. *The Journal of Asian Studies*, 32(4), 639–59.

Klein, I. (1988). Plague, policy and popular unrest in British India. *Modern Asian Studies*, 22(4), 723–55. https://doi.org/10.1017/S0026749X00015729

Kolata, G. (2020). How pandemics end. *The New York Times*, May 10. www.nytimes.com/2020/05/10/health/coronavirus-plague-pandemic-history.html (accessed September 2020).

Kraut, A. M. (2010). Immigration, ethnicity, and the pandemic. *Public Health Reports*, 125(3), 123–33. https://doi.org/10.1177/00333549101250S315

Ladurie, E. L. (1981). *The Mind and Method of the Historian*. Chicago: Chicago University Press.

Langford, C. (2002). The age pattern of mortality in the 1918–19 influenza pandemic: an attempted explanation based on data for England and Wales. *Medical History*, 46(1), 1–20.

Langford, C. (2005). Did the 1918–19 influenza pandemic originate in China? *Population and Development Review*, 31(3), 473–505. https://doi.org/10.1111/j.1728-4457.2005.00080.x

Langford, C. M. & Storey, P. (1992). Influenza in Sri Lanka, 1918–1919: The impact of a new disease in a premier third world setting. *Health Transition Review*, 2(1), 97–123.

Lee, V. J., Chen, M. I., Chan, S. P. et al. (2007). Influenza pandemics in Singapore, a tropical, globally connected city. *Emerging Infectious Diseases*, 13(7), 1052–57. https://doi.org/10.1111/j.1728-4457.2005.00080.x

Lewis, W. A. (1954). Economic development with unlimited supplies of labour. *The Manchester School*, 22(2), 139–91. https://doi.org/10.1111/j.1467-9957.1954.tb00021.x

Liew, K. K. (2007). Terribly severe though mercifully short: The episode of the 1918 influenza in British Malaya. *Modern Asian Studies*, 41(2), 221–52. https://doi.org/10.1017/S0026749X05002180

Lilley, A., Lilley, M., & G. Rinaldi, G. (2020). Public health interventions and economic growth: Revisiting the Spanish flu evidence. *Available at SSRN 3590008* (2020).

Lim, C. (2011). The pandemic of the Spanish influenza in colonial Korea. *Korea Journal*, 51(4), 59–88. https://doi.org/10.25024/kj.2011.51.4.59

Lin, M.-J. & Liu, E. M. (2014). Does in *Utero* exposure to illness matter? The 1918 influenza epidemic in Taiwan as a natural experiment. *Journal of Health Economics*, 37(1), 152–63. https://doi.org/10.1016/j.jhealeco.2014.05.004

Mamelund, S.-E. (2004). Can the Spanish influenza pandemic of 1918 explain the baby boom of 1920 in neutral Norway? *Population*, 59(2), 229–60. https://doi.org/10.2307/3654904

Mamelund, S.-E. (2006). A socially neutral disease? individual social class, household wealth and mortality from Spanish influenza in two socially contrasting parishes in Kristiania 1918–19. *Social Science & Medicine*, 62(4), 923–40. https://doi.org/10.1016/j.socscimed.2005.06.051

Mamelund, S. E. (2018). 1918 pandemic morbidity: The first wave hits the poor, the second wave hits the rich. *Influenza Other Respiratory Viruses*, 12(3), 307–13.

Markel, H., Lipman, H. B., Navarro, J. A. et al. (2007). Non pharmaceutical interventions implemented by US cities during the 1918–19 influenza pandemic. *Journal of the American Medical Association*, 298(6), 644–54. https://doi.org/10.1001/jama.298.6.644

McBride, T. (1976). The domestic revolution: The modernization of household service in England and France, 1820–1920. New York: Holmes and Meier.

McQueen, H. (1976), The 'Spanish' influenza pandemic in Australia, 1918–19. In J. Roe, ed., *Social Policy in Australia*, Melbourne: Melbourne University Press, pp. 131–47

The Medical Journal of Australia (MJA) (1919). Influenza and medical quarantined. *MJA*, August, 2(8), 160–2. https://doi.org/10.5694/j.1326-5377.1919.tb52403.x

Mills, I. D. (1986). The 1918–1919 influenza pandemic: The Indian experience. *The Indian Economic & Social History Review*, 23(1), 1–40. https://doi.org/10.1177/001946468602300102

Ministry of Health, U.K. (1920). Report on the Pandemic of Influenza, 1918–19. *Reports on Health and Medical Subjects No. 4*. London: Her Majesty's Stationery Office (as cited in Mills, 1986).Health, U.K., Report on the Pandemic of Influenza, 1918–19, 4, HMSO, 1920, p. 182.

Morens, D. M. & Fauci, A. S. (2007). The 1918 influenza pandemic: Insights for the 21st Century. *The Journal of Infectious Diseases*, 195(7), 1018–28. https://doi.org/10.1086/511989h

Morens, D. M., Taubenberger, J. K., & Fauci, A. S. (2021). A centenary tale of two pandemics: The 1918 influenza pandemic and COVID-19. *American Journal of Public Health*, 111(6), 1086–94 (Part 1) and June 10. https://doi.org/10.2105/AJPH.2021.306326 (part 2).

Morton-Jack, G. (2018). *Army of Empire: The Untold Story of the Indian Army in World War I*. New York: Basic Books.

Moxnes, J. F. & Christophersen, O. A. (2008). The Spanish flu as a worst case scenario? *Microbial Ecology in Health and Disease*, 20(1), 1–26. https://doi.org/10.1080/08910600701699067

Murray, C. J. L., Lopez, A. D., Chin, B., Feehan, D. & Hill, K. H. (2006). Estimation of potential global pandemic influenza mortality on the basis of vital registry data from the 1918–20 pandemic: A quantitative analysis. *The Lancet*, 368(9554), 2211–8. https://doi.org/10.1016/S0140-6736(06)69895-4

Myrskylä, M., Mehta, N. K., & Chang, V. W. (2013). Early life exposure to the 1918 influenza pandemic and old-age mortality by cause of death. *American Journal of Public Health*, 103(7), e83–e90.

National Museum of Australia (undated). Defining moments: Influenza pandemic. www.nma.gov.au/defining-moments/resources/influenza-pandemic (accessed 25 May 2021).

Neelsen, S. & T. Stratmann, T. (2012). Long-run effects of fetal influenza exposure: Evidence from Switzerland. *Social Science & Medicine*, 74(1), 58–66. https://doi.org/10.1016/j.socscimed.2011.09.039

Nelson, R. E. (2010). Testing the fetal origins hypothesis in a developing country: Evidence from the 1918 influenza pandemic. *Health Economics*, 19(10), 1181–92. https://doi.org/10.1002/hec.1544

Nickol, M. E. & Kindrachuk, J. (2019). A year of terror and a century of reflection: perspectives on the great influenza pandemic of 1918–1919. *BMC Infectious Disease*, 9(1),117–26. https://doi.org/10.1186/s12879-019-3750-8

Nitisastro, W. (1970). *Population Trends in Indonesia*. Ithaca: Cornell University Press.

Noy, I., Okubo, T. and Strobl, E. (2020). The Japanese textile sector and the influenza pandemic of 1918–1920. *CESifo Working Paper No. 8651*. Munich: CESif Group. http://hdl.handle.net/10419/229469

Noymer, A. (2011). The 1918 influenza pandemic hastened the decline of tuberculosis in the United States: an age, period, cohort analysis. *Vaccine*, 29, B38–B41.

Ogburn, W. F. & Thomas, D. S. (1922). The Influence of the business cycle on certain social conditions. *Journal of the American Statistical Association*, 18(139), 324–40.

Ogasawara, K. (2018). The long-run effects of pandemic influenza on the development of children from elite backgrounds: Evidence from industrializing Japan. *Economics and Human Biology*, 31, 125–37.

Ohadike, D. C. (1981). The influenza pandemic of 1918–19 and the spread of cassava cultivation on the lower Niger: a study in historical linkages. *The Journal of African History*, 22(3), 379–91.

Ohadike, D. C. (1991). Diffusion and physiological responses to the influenza pandemic of 1918–19 in Nigeria. *Social Science & Medicine*, 32(12), 1393–9. https://doi.org/10.1016/0277-9536(91)90200-V

Oluwasegun, J. M. (2017). Managing epidemic: the British approach to 1918–1919 influenza in Lagos. *Journal of Asian and African Studies*, 52(4), 412–24.

Økland, H. & Mamelund, S. (2019). Race and 1918 influenza pandemic in the United States: a review of the literature. *International Journal of Environmental research and Public Health*, 16(14), 2487–505.

Osterholm, M. T. (2005). Preparing for the next pandemic. *Foreign Affairs*, 84(4), 24–37.

Osterholm, M. T. & Olshakar, M. (2017). *Deadliest Enemy: Our War Against Killer German*. New York: Little Brown.

Osterholm, M. T. & Olshaker, M. (2020). Chronicle of a pandemic foretold. *Foreign Affairs*, 99(10), 18–24.

Ott, M., Shaw, S. F., Danila, R. N., & Lynfield, R. (2007). Lessons learned from the 1918–1919 influenza pandemic in Minneapolis and St. Paul, Minnesota. *Public Health Reports*, 122(6), 803–10.

Oxford, J. S. (2001). The so-called great Spanish influenza pandemic of 1918 may have originated in France in 1916. *Philosophical Transactions of the Royal Society of London. Series B: Biological Sciences*, 356(416), 1857–9.

Oxford, J. S. Sefton, A., Jackson, R. et al. (2002). World War I may have allowed the emergence of 'Spanish' influenza. *The Lancet Infectious Diseases*, 2(2), 111–4.

Pankhurst, R. (1977). A historical note on influenza in Ethiopia. *Medical History*, 21(2), 195–200. https://doi.org/10.1017/S002572730003773X

Patterson, K. D. (1983). The influenza epidemic of 1918–19 in the Gold Coast. *The Journal of African History*, 24(4), 485–502. https://doi.org/10.1017/S0021853700028012

Patterson, K. D. & Pyle, G. F. (1983). The diffusion of influenza in Sub-Saharan Africa during the 1918–1919 Pandemic. *Social Science & Medicine*, 17(17), 1299–307. https://doi.org/10.1016/0277-9536(83)90022-9

Patterson, K. D. & Pyle, G. F. (1991). The Geography and mortality of the 1918 influenza pandemic. *Bulletin of the History of Medicine*, 65(1), 4–21.

Percoco, M. (2016). Health shocks and human capital accumulation: the case of Spanish flu in Italian regions. *Regional Studies*, 50(9), 1496–508.

Petersen, E., Koopmans, M., Go, U. et al. (2020). Comparing SARS-CoV-2 with influenza pandemics. *The Lancet Infectious Diseases*, 20, e238–e344.

Pettit, D. A. & Bailie, P. (2008). *A cruel wind: Pandemic Influenza in America, 1918–1920*. Murfreesboro, TN: Timberlane Books.

Phillips, H. (1988). South Africa's worst demographic disaster: The Spanish influenza epidemic of 1918. *South African Historical Journal*, 20(1), 57–73.

Phillips, H. (2004). The Re-appearing shadow of 1918: Trends in the historiography of the 1918–19 influenza pandemic. *Canadian Bulletin of Medical History*, 21(1), 121–34. https://doi.org/10.3138/cbmh.21.1.121

Phillips, H. (2014). The recent wave of 'Spanish' flu historiography. *Social History of Medicine*, 27(4), 789–808.

Phillips, H. (2017). Influenza pandemic (Africa). In U. P. Daniel, O. Gatrell, H. Janz. J. Jones, J. Keene, A. Kramer & B. Nasson, eds., *Encyclopedia of the First World War*, Berlin: Freie Universität Berlin, pp. 1/12–11/12. https://encyclopedia .1914-1918-online.net/pdf/1914-1918-Online-influenza_pandemic_africa-2014-10-08.pdf

Phipson, E. S. (1923). The pandemic of influenza in India in the year 1918. *The Indian Medical Gazette*, 58(11), 509–24.

Pool, D. I. (1973). The Effects of the 1918 pandemic of influenza on the Maori population of New Zealand. *Bulletin of the History of Medicine*, 47(3), 273–81.

Ramusack, B. (2004). *The Indian Princes and Their States, The New Cambridge History of India, III 6*. Cambridge: Cambridge University Press.

Ranger, T. (1992). The Influenza pandemic in Southern Rhodesia: A crisis of comprehension. In D. Arnold, ed., *Imperial Medicine and Indigenous Societies*, Manchester: Manchester University Press, Chapter 10, pp. 172–88.

Ranger, T. (2003). A Historian's foreword. In H. Phillips & D. Killingray, eds., *The Spanish Influenza Pandemic of 1918–19: New Perspectives*. London: Routledge, pp. xx–xxi.

Reyes, O., Lee, E. C., Sah, P. et al. (2018). Spatiotemporal patterns and diffusion of the 1918 influenza pandemic in British India. *American Journal of Epidemiology*, 187(12), 2550–60. https://doi.org/10.1093/aje kwy209

Rice, G. W. (1988). *Black November: The 1918 Influenza Pandemic in New Zealand*. Wellington: Allen & Unwin.

Rice, G. W. (2003). Japan and New Zealand in the 1918 influenza pandemic: Comparative perspectives on official responses and crisis management.

In H. Phillip and D. Killingray, eds., *The Spanish Flu Pandemic of 1918: New Perspectives*. London: Routledge, pp.73–95.

Richard, S. A., Sugaya, N., Simonsen, L., Miller, M. A., & Viboud, C. (2009). A Comparative study of the 1918–1920 influenza pandemic in Japan, USA and UK: Mortality impact and implications for pandemic planning. *Epidemiology & Infection*, 137(8), 1062–72. https://doi.org/10.1017/S0950268809002088

Roes, F. (2018). The curious case of the Spanish Flu. *Biological Theory*, 13(4), 243–5. https://doi.org/10.1007/s13752-018-0307-9

Rose, C. S. (2021). Implications of the Spanish influenza pandemic (1918–1920) for the history of early 20th century Egypt. *Journal of World History*, 32(4), 655–84.

Rosen, G. (2015). *A History of Public Health*. Baltimore: Johns Hopkins University Press.

Royal Thai Government. (1919). *Ratchakitchanubeksa 1919*, 36, 1193–1202 [in Thai]. www.ratchakitcha.soc.go.th/DATA/PDF/2462/D/1193.PDF

Sambala, E. Z. (2012). Diffusion, mortality and responses to pandemic influenza in Nyasaland, 1918–1920. *South African Historical Journal*, 73(1), 45–63.

Sekher, T. V. (2021). Influenza pandemic of 1918. *Economic & Political Weekly*, 56(21), 32–8.

Scheidel, W. (2017). *The Great Levers: Violence and the History of Inequality from Stone Age to the Twenty-First Century*, Princeton: Princeton University Press. https://doi.org/10.1515/9781400884605

Schultz, T. W. (1964). *Transforming Traditional Agriculture*. New Haven: Yale University Press.

Sen, A. K. (1967). Surplus labour in India: A critique of Schultz's statistical test. *The Economic Journal*, 77(305), 154–61. https://doi.org/10.2307/2229374

Sen, A. K. (1992). Missing women. *British Medical Journal*, 304(6827), 587. https://doi.org/10.1136/bmj.304.6827.587

Sen, R. K. (1923). *A Treatise on Influenza with special Reference to the Pandemic of 1918*. North Lakhimpur, Assam.

Sencer, D. J. & Millar, J. D. (2006). Reflections on the 1976 Swine Flu vaccination program. *Emerging Infectious Diseases*, 12(1), 29–33. https://doi.org/10.3201/eid1201.051007

Shanks, G. D. (2018). The influenza vaccine used during the Samoan Pandemic of 1918. *Tropical Medicine and Infectious Diseases*, 3(1), 17–22.

Shanks, G. D. & Brundage, J. F. (2013). Pacific islands which escaped the 1918–1919 influenza pandemic and their subsequent mortality experiences. *Epidemiology & Infection*, 141(2), 353–6.

Shortridge, K. F. (1999). The 1918 Spanish flu: pearls from swine? *Nature Medicine*, 5(4), 384–5.

Słomczyński, S. (2012). There are sick people everywhere in cities, towns and villages: The course of the Spanish flu epidemic in Poland. *Roczniki Dziejów Społecznych i Gospodarczych*, 72(1), 74–92. https://doi.org/10.12775/RDSG.2012.03

Spinney, L. (2017). *Pale River: The Spanish Flu of 1918 and How it Changed the World*. New Yok: Public Affairs.

Steinberg, G. W. (2002). Material conditions, knowledge and trade in Central Asia during the 19th and early 20th centuries. *Working Paper RSC 2002/16*. San Domenico, Italy: European University Institution.

Stiglitz, J. E., Jayadev, A., & Prabhala, A. (2020). Patents vs. the Pandemic. *Project Syndicate*. www.project-syndicate.org/commentary/covid19-drugs-and-vaccine-demand-patent-reform-by-joseph-e-stiglitz-et-al-2020-04 (accessed September 2020).

Strachan, H. (2004). *The First World War in Africa*. Oxford: Oxford University Press.

Sydenstricker, E. (1931). The incidence of influenza among persons of different economic status during the epidemic of 1918. *Public Health Reports (1896–1970)*, 46(4), 154–70. https://doi.org/10.2307/4579923

Taubenberger, J. K. (2003). Genetic characterization of the 1918 'Spanish' influenza virus. In H. Phillip & D. Killingray, eds., *The Spanish Flu Pandemic of 1918: New Perspectives*. London: Routledge, pp. 39–51.

Taubenberger, J. K., Hultin, J. V., & Morens, D. M. (2007). Discovery and characterization of the 1918 pandemic influenza virus in historical context. *Antiviral Therapy*, 12(4), 581–91.

Taubenberger, J. K. & Morens, D. M. (2006). 1918 influenza virus: The mother of all pandemics. *Emerging Infectious Diseases*, 2(1), 15–22. https://doi.org/10.3201/eid1209.05-0979

Taubenberger, J. K. & Morens, D. M. (2020). The 1918 influenza pandemic and its legacy. *Cold Spring Harbor Perspectives in Medicine*, 10(10), a038695.

Thongcharoen, P. (2017). A chronical outbreak of influenza in Thailand. *Outbreak, Surveillance and Investigation Report*, 10(4), 24–6 (Ministry of Public Health, Thailand).

Tomkins, S. M. (1992). The influenza epidemic of 1918–19 in Western Samoa. *The Journal of Pacific History*, 27(2), 181–97. https://doi.org/10.1080/00223349208572706

Tomkins, S. M. (1994). Colonial administration in British Africa during the influenza epidemic of 1918–19. *Canadian Journal of African Studies*, 28(1), 60–83. https://doi.org/10.2307/485825

Tsoucalas, G., Kousoulis, A., & Sgantzos, M. (2016). The 1918 Spanish flu pandemic, the origins of the H1N1-virus strain, a glance in history. *European Journal of Clinical and Biomedical Sciences*, 2(4), 23–8.

The Economist. (2018). A Deadly Touch of Flu. 29 September, 68–70. http://article.ejcbs.org/html/10.11648.j.ejcbs.20160204.11.html.

The Economist. (2020a). How the Spanish flu of 1918–20 was largely forgotten. *The Economist*, 18 April 2020. www.economist.com/international/2020/04/18/how-the-spanish-flu-of-1918-20-was-largely-forgotten.

The Economist. (2020b). Why relations between economists and epidemiologists have been testy. *The Economist*, 12 November 2020. www.economist.com/finance-and-economics/2020/11/14/why-relations-between-economists-and-epidemiologists-have-been-testy.

van der Eng, P. (2020). Mortality from the influenza pandemic of 1918–19 in Indonesia: A comment in the context of the COVID-19 pandemic. Unpublished manuscript, School of Economics and Business, Australian National University.

Velde, F. R. (2020). What happened to the US economy during the 1918 influenza pandemic? A view through high-frequency data. *Working Paper 2020–11*, Federal Reserve Bank of Chicago.

Viboud, C., Eisenstein, J., Reid, A. H. et al. (2013). Age-and sex-specific mortality associated with the 1918–1919 influenza pandemic in Kentucky. *The Journal of Infectious Diseases*, 207(5), 721–9. https://doi.org/10.1093/infdis/jis745

Wakimura, K. (1966). Famines, epidemics and mortality in northern India, 1870–1921. In R. Robb, K. Sugihara & H. Yanigisawa, eds., *Local Agrarian Societies in Colonial India: Japanese Perspectives*. London: Manohar, pp. 287–8.

Wang, C., Horby, P. W., Hayden, F. G., & Gao, G. F. (2020). A Novel coronavirus outbreak of global health concern. *The Lancet*, 395(10223), 470–3. https://doi.org/10.1016/S0140-6736(20)30185-9

Wever, P. C. & Van Bergen. L. (2014). Death from 1918 pandemic influenza during the first World War: A perspective from personal and anecdotal evidence. *Influenza and Other Respiratory Viruses*, 8(5), 538–46. https://doi.org/10.1111/irv.12267

Wibowo, P. & associates. (2009). *Pandemic Influenza 1918 Di Hindia Belanda*. Depok: UNICEF Jakarta/Komnas FBPI.

Wilson, J. (2016). *India Conquered: Britain's Raj and the Chaos of Empire.* New York: Simon and Schuster.

Woolhouse, M. E. J., Webster, J. P., Domingo, E., Charlesworth, B. & Levin, B. R. (2002). Biological and biomedical implications of the co-evolution of pathogens and their hosts. *Nature Genetics*, 32(4), 569–77. https://doi.org/10.1038/ng1202-569

World Economic Forum. (2020). How Can We Save Lives and the Economy? Lessons from the Spanish Flu Pandemic. Geneva: World Economic Forum. www.weforum.org/agenda/2020/04/pandemic-economy-lessons-1918-flu (accessed September 2020).

Yaylymova, A. (2020). COVID-19 in Turkmenistan: No data, no health rights. *Health and Human Right Journal*, 22(2), 325–8. www.hhrjournal.org/2020/10/covid-19-in-turkmenistan-no-data-no-health-rights/.

Acknowledgements

In the process of undertaking this study we have received invaluable help from a number of people. Sisira Jayasuriya stimulated our interest in this subject. Wishnu Mahraddhika and Wannaphong Durogkaveroj helped us in accessing Indonesian- and Thai-language literature, respectively. Soma Athukorala helped with literature search and accessing material from the National Library of Australia. Tilak Abeysinghe guided us in the interpretation of pandemic mortality figures based on alternative estimation methods. At the formative stage of our research, we received valuable comments and suggestions from Hal Hill, Ross McLeod, Peter Warr, Jayant Menon and other participants of the *Trade and Development Seminar* in the Arndt-Corden Department of Economics, Australian National University. Tony Thirlwall carefully read the entire penultimate version of the manuscript and made wise comments. The two anonymous CUP reviewers made incisive comments that led to major elaborations of some slighted issues. Tony Addison and Kunal Sen at WIDER steered this project to its completion with patience and perseverance. We sincerely thank them all.

Cambridge Elements ☰

Development Economics

Series Editor-in-Chief

Kunal Sen
UNU-WIDER, and University of Manchester

Kunal Sen, UNU-WIDER Director, is Editor-in-Chief of the Cambridge Elements in Development Economics series. Professor Sen has over three decades of experience in academic and applied development economics research, and has carried out extensive work on international finance, the political economy of inclusive growth, the dynamics of poverty, social exclusion, female labour force participation, and the informal sector in developing economies. His research has focused on India, East Asia, and sub-Saharan Africa.

In addition to his work as Professor of Development Economics at the University of Manchester, Kunal has been the Joint Research Director of the Effective States and Inclusive Development (ESID) Research Centre, and a Research Fellow at the Institute for Labor Economics (IZA). He has also served in advisory roles with national governments and bilateral and multilateral development agencies, including the UK's Department for International Development, Asian Development Bank, and the International Development Research Centre.

Thematic Editors

Tony Addison
University of Copenhagen, and UNU-WIDER

Tony Addison is a Professor of Economics in the University of Copenhagen's Development Economics Research Group. He is also a Non-Resident Senior Research Fellow at UNU-WIDER, Helsinki, where he was previously the Chief Economist-Deputy Director. In addition, he is Professor of Development Studies at the University of Manchester. His research interests focus on the extractive industries, energy transition, and macroeconomic policy for development.

Chris Barret
Johnson College of Business, Cornell University

Chris Barrett is an agricultural and development economist at Cornell University. He is the Stephen B. and Janice G. Ashley Professor of Applied Economics and Management; and International Professor of Agriculture at the Charles H. Dyson School of Applied Economics and Management. He is also an elected Fellow of the American Association for the Advancement of Science, the Agricultural and Applied Economics Association, and the African Association of Agricultural Economists.

Carlos Gradín
UNU-WIDER, and University of Vigo

Carlos Gradín is a UNU-WIDER Research Fellow, and a professor of applied economics at the University of Vigo (on leave). His main research interest is the study of inequalities, with special attention to those that exist between population groups (e.g., by race or sex). His publications have contributed to improving the empirical evidence in developing and developed countries, as well as globally, and to improving the available data and methods used.

Rachel M. Gisselquist
UNU-WIDER

Rachel M. Gisselquist is a Senior Research Fellow and member of the Senior Management Team of UNU-WIDER. She specializes in the comparative politics of developing countries, with particular attention to issues of inequality, ethnic and identity politics, foreign aid and state building, democracy and governance, and sub-Saharan African politics. Dr Gisselquist has edited a dozen collections in these areas, and her articles are published in a range of leading journals.

Shareen Joshi
Georgetown University

Shareen Joshi is an Associate Professor of International Development at Georgetown University's School of Foreign Service in the United States. Her research focuses on issues of inequality, human capital investment and grassroots collective action in South Asia. Her work has been published in the fields of development economics, population studies, environmental studies and gender studies.

Patricia Justino
Senior Research Fellow, UNU-WIDER, and IDS – UK

Patricia Justino is a Senior Research Fellow at UNU-WIDER and Professorial Fellow at the Institute of Development Studies (IDS) (on leave). Her research focuses on the relationship between political violence, governance and development outcomes. She has published widely in the fields of development economics and political economy and is the co-founder and co-director of the Households in Conflict Network (HiCN).

Marinella Leone
University of Pavia

Marinella Leone is an assistant professor at the Department of Economics and Management, University of Pavia, Italy. She is an applied development economist. Her more recent research focuses on the study of early child development parenting programmes, on education, and gender-based violence. In previous research she investigated the short-, long-term and intergenerational impact of conflicts on health, education and domestic violence. She has published in top journals in economics and development economics.

Jukka Pirttilä
University of Helsinki, and UNU-WIDER

Jukka Pirttilä is Professor of Public Economics at the University of Helsinki and VATT Institute for Economic Research. He is also a Non-Resident Senior Research Fellow at UNU-WIDER. His research focuses on tax policy, especially for developing countries. He is a co-principal investigator at the Finnish Centre of Excellence in Tax Systems Research.

Andy Sumner
King's College London, and UNU-WIDER

Andy Sumner is Professor of International Development at King's College London; a Non-Resident Senior Fellow at UNU-WIDER and a Fellow of the Academy of Social Sciences. He has published extensively in the areas of poverty, inequality, and economic development.

About the Series

Cambridge Elements in Development Economics is led by UNU-WIDER in partnership with Cambridge University Press. The series publishes authoritative studies on important topics in the field covering both micro and macro aspects of development economics.

United Nations University World Institute for Development Economics Research

United Nations University World Institute for Development Economics Research (UNU-WIDER) provides economic analysis and policy advice aiming to promote sustainable and equitable development for all. The institute began operations in 1985 in Helsinki, Finland, as the first research centre of the United Nations University. Today, it is one of the world's leading development economics think tanks, working closely with a vast network of academic researchers and policy makers, mostly based in the Global South.

UNITED NATIONS
UNIVERSITY
UNU-WIDER

Cambridge Elements ☰

Development Economics

Printed in the United States
by Baker & Taylor Publisher Services